CHOUX TEMPTATIONS

Jialin Tian, Ph.D.

Photographs and Design by Jialin Tian
Step-by-Step Photographs by Yabin Yu

Choux Temptations

Jialin Tian, Ph.D.

Published in the United States by
Jayca Inc.
P. O. Box 2451
Poquoson, VA 23662
USA

Photographs and styling: Jialin Tian
Step-by-step photographs and author's photographs: Yabin Yu
Book design: Jialin Tian
Production manager: Yabin Yu

www.macaronmagic.com

ISBN 978-0-9837764-3-7

First Edition

CONTENTS

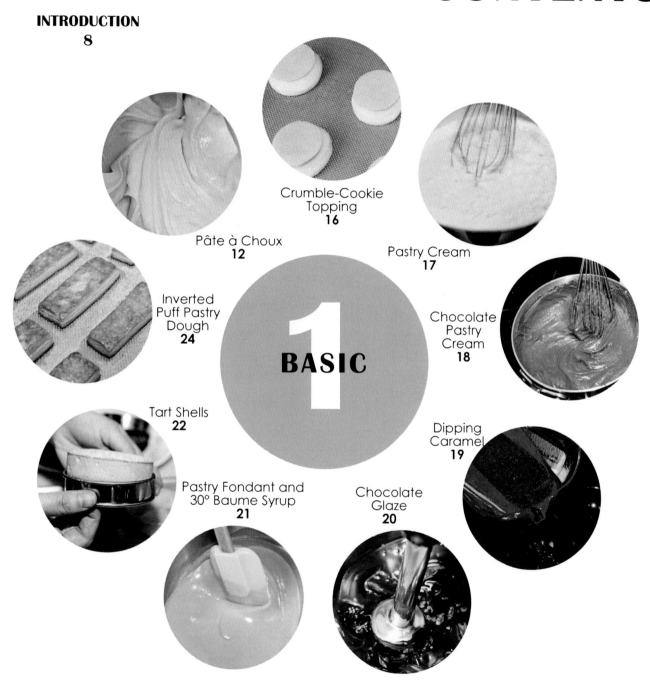

2
CLASSIC

Raspberry and Lychee Mascarpone
54

Peanut Butter and Caramelized Banana
64

Espresso and Chocolate
57

Calamansi and Blackberry
60

Blueberry, Meyer Lemon, and Oats
70

Pineapple and Guava
67

CONTEMPORARY
3

Walnut and Chocolate
74

Apricot and Almond Mascarpone
78

Pistachio and Strawberry
82

Wild West (Red Bean Paste)
106

Bunny (Carrot Cream-Cheese)
88

Scholar (Jasmine Tea)
92

FUNNY
4

The Son of Chou
(Green Apple Mascarpone
and Caramel)
102

Santa (Chestnuts)
98

Witch (Pumpkin Mascarpone)
95

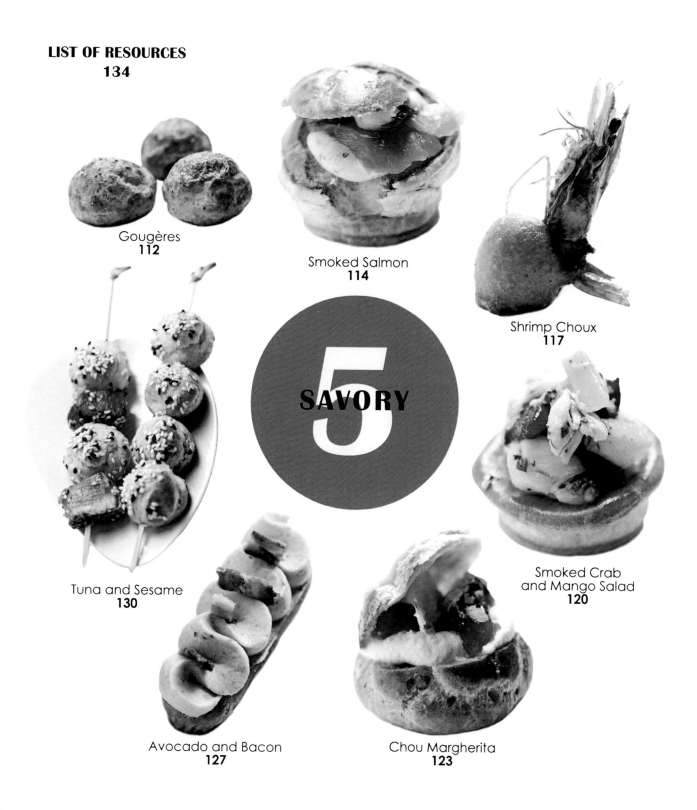

Gougères
112

Smoked Salmon
114

Shrimp Choux
117

5

SAVORY

Tuna and Sesame
130

Smoked Crab
and Mango Salad
120

Avocado and Bacon
127

Chou Margherita
123

INTRODUCTION

Light, airy, and crispy, the versatile choux have been delighting pastry enthusiasts for centuries. The word chou(x) means cabbage(s) in French. Baked choux are shaped like cabbages, hence the origin of the name. According to culinary historians, the ingenious choux pastry originated in Renaissance Italy and was later introduced to France by Catherine de' Medici. The modern version of the choux pastry was created by famed French chef Antonin Carême in the nineteenth century. Since then, this remarkable baking method has given us beloved French classics such as éclairs, profiteroles, Paris-Brest, Religieuses, St. Honorés, and more. Today, a new generation of pastry creators continues to dazzle us with an array of innovative choux creations. As the timeless classics are being reinvented, brand new choux pastries are developed to tempt pastry lovers in today's trendy pastry scene.

This book is a celebration of the beloved choux. The book is divided into five chapters. The first chapter contains the basic recipes that are used throughout the book. The fundamental technique of the dual-cooking process for preparing pâte à choux (choux paste) is introduced. In addition, this chapter discusses the multi-stage baking approach that helps to solve a common problem in baking choux. In the second chapter, we revisit the techniques for creating some of the best-known French classic choux pastries. In chapter three, we focus on contemporary choux creations. With a variety of techniques, components, ingredients, and textures, these elegant works of art truly showcase the brilliance of the choux pastry. Inspired by the classic Religieuse, in chapter four, we present several whimsical choux characters that are absolute delights. Finally, in chapter five, we demonstrate the versatility of choux pastry in several savory creations. Although most creations in the book employ the traditional ingredients used in the classic preparation method, several recipes in chapters three and five include novel ingredients such as olive oil, oats, and walnut oil in the basic choux preparation to emphasize the healthier aspect of modern pastry.

Choux Temptations contains instructions for creating thirty sophisticated and innovative choux pastries. Each recipe is accompanied by step-by-step photographs as well as photographs of finished works. The complexity of the recipes ranges from intermediate to advanced. I have found the most effective method to tackle a complicated recipe composed of multiple elements is to understand the concept of the component-oriented approach. For instance, if someone can master the techniques for preparing the individual recipes presented in the first chapter, then he or she should be able to handle any of the more complicated recipes in the book. In addition, it is essential to plan ahead; clear organization and detailed scheduling are the keys to success. Furthermore, it is also helpful to read and understand the recipe in its entirety, then try to visualize each step, and finally carry out the procedures.

This is my fourth cookbook collaboration with my mother, Yabin. As always, she has made tremendous contributions to this work. During the creation of this book, we have grown closer and I have learned to appreciate her more than ever. Always thinking in synchronization, we also discovered that we have so much in common in so many ways other than just in engineering and science. I also want thank my father, Richard, for his valuable contribution and support; together we make a wonderful team. In addition, I wish to express my deepest appreciation to all the pastry professionals and enthusiasts for their precious support, feedback, and encouragement! I could not have done it without you!

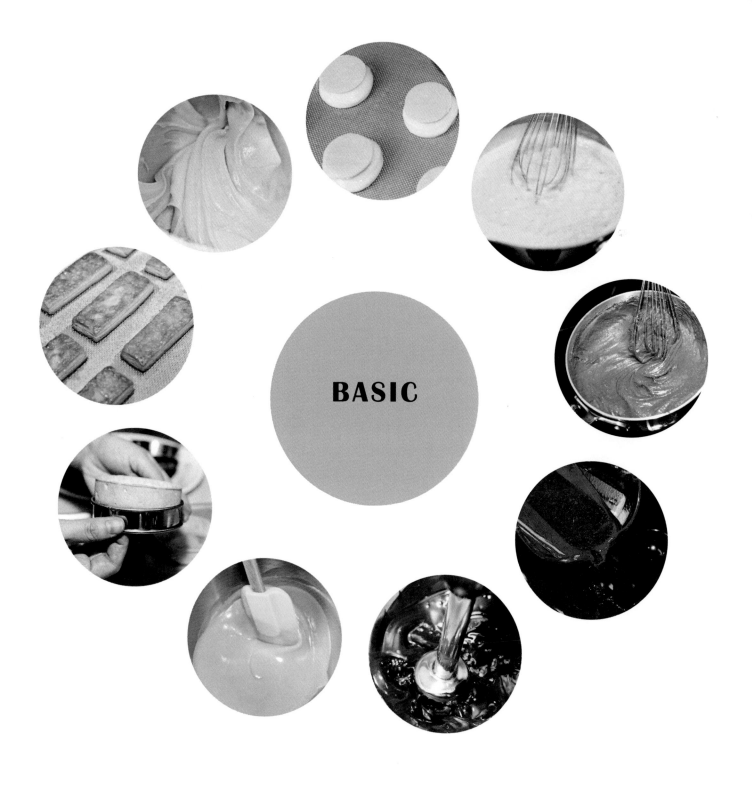

BASIC

PÂTE À CHOUX

Pâte à choux, or choux paste, is the principal component for making any choux pastry. When properly made, baked choux should be light, airy, and moist on the inside and slightly crispy on the outside. Choux pastries require a dual cooking process. During the first stage, a thick paste is made from flour, liquid, and fat components. In the second stage, eggs are beaten into the cooked paste to produce a thinner paste, which is shaped and baked into the desired form. Steam is the only leavening agent in the choux paste. As the water in the paste evaporates during baking, it creates steam. Because the initial cooking stage activates the gluten, thus strengthening the starch bond in the paste, the steam is trapped inside the paste. As a result, the pastry is lifted to several times its original volume. It is this unique process that gives the choux pastry its signature characteristics. However, sometimes baked choux tend to cave in on the bottom or even collapse onto themselves, which is a common problem caused by rapid air cooling. During baking, the air inside the choux expands as the temperature increases. However, when the choux are removed from the hot oven, the temperature drops rapidly, which creates an imbalance in air pressure between the interior and exterior of the choux. As a result, the choux collapse.

Luckily, this problem can be easily solved. To avoid the cave-in phenomenon in baking pâte à choux, we employ a three-stage baking process that includes a rapid rising stage, a baking stage, and a gradual cooling period. In the first phase, choux are baked at a high temperature; during this period, the steam in the choux paste helps to increase the choux volume significantly. In the second phase, the temperature is reduced to allow sufficient baking to occur. Finally, in the last phase, the oven is turned off; the choux are cooled gradually to avoid collapse.

Yield: about 540 g/19 oz choux pastry paste

INGREDIENTS

120 g/4.2 oz all-purpose flour

100 g/3.5 oz distilled water

100 g/3.5 oz whole milk

2 g/0.071 oz (¼ tsp) kosher salt or fine sea salt

5 g/0.18 oz (1 tsp) granulated sugar

80 g/2.8 oz unsalted butter

200 g/7.1 oz whole eggs (about 4 eggs)

1 whole egg for egg wash

Preparing the Choux Paste:

1. Sift the flour onto a piece of parchment paper [1]. Transfer the sifted flour to a bowl and reserve.

2. Combine the water, milk, salt, sugar, and butter in a large stainless steel saucepan; heat the mixture over medium-high heat [2].

3. When the mixture comes to a boil, remove the saucepan from heat. Carefully whisk the sifted flour into the mixture [3–6]. When all the flour is incorporated into the liquid, shake off lumps of dough from the whisk and switch to a spatula or wooden spoon [7].

4. Return the saucepan to medium-low heat. Continue to cook for 2 to 3 minutes; stir constantly, using a folding motion to eliminate any remaining

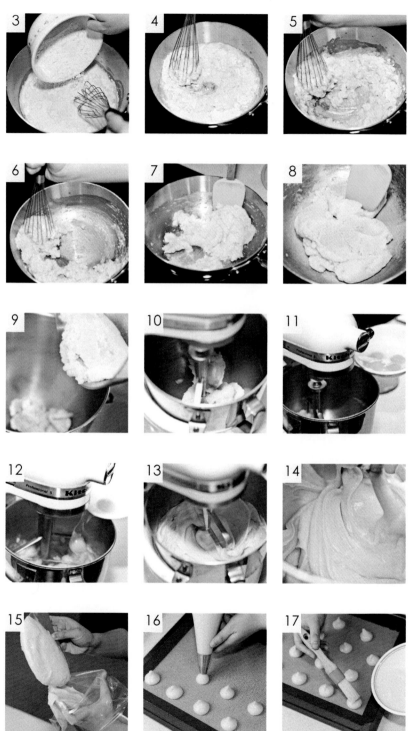

small lumps of flour and bring the dough pieces together. Cook until a smooth and thick paste is obtained [8].

5. Transfer the dough to a mixer bowl [9]. Attach the bowl to a mixer fitted with a paddle attachment. Mix the dough at medium speed for 10 to 15 seconds to release the steam [10].

6. Add the eggs one at a time while continuing to mix on medium speed [11, 12]. Make sure each egg is incorporated before adding additional eggs. Scrape down the sides of the mixer bowl with a spatula if necessary. Increase the mixer speed to high. Mix for 10 to 20 seconds or until a smooth paste forms [13, 14].

7. Meanwhile, line a half-sheet baking pan with a silicone baking mat or parchment paper.

Baking the Choux:

For 3.8-cm/1.5-in round mini choux (makes about 60):

1. Preheat the oven to 191°C/375°F. Fill a large pastry bag (45.7-cm/18-in) fitted with a 1.3-cm/0.5-in plain tip (#806) with the choux paste [15]. Pipe the paste into 2.5-cm/1-in mounds with 2.5-cm/1-in spacing on the baking mat or parchment paper [16]. Brush the top with egg wash using a gentle dabbing motion [17].

2. Bake at 191°C/375°F for about 13 minutes until the choux are puffed up [18]. Reduce the temperature to 177°C/350°F and bake for another 13 minutes until the choux are golden brown. Turn off the oven and leave the choux in the oven undisturbed for another 8 minutes. Remove the baked choux from the oven and let cool completely [19–21].

For 5-cm/2-in round small choux (makes about 30):

1. Preheat the oven to 191°C/375°F. Fill a large pastry bag (45.7-cm/18-in) fitted with a 1.7-cm/0.69-in plain tip (#809) with the choux paste. Pipe the

paste into 3.8-cm/1.5-in mounds with 2.5-cm/1-in spacing on the baking mat or parchment paper. Brush the top with egg wash using a gentle dabbing motion.

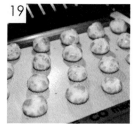

2. Bake at 191°C/375°F for about 17 minutes until the choux are puffed up. Reduce the temperature to 177°C/350°F and bake for another 15 minutes until the choux are golden brown. Turn off the oven and leave the choux in the oven undisturbed for another 10 minutes. Remove the baked choux from the oven and let cool completely.

For 6.4-cm/2.5-in round medium-sized choux (makes about 18):

1. Preheat the oven to 191°C/375°F. Fill a large pastry bag (45.7-cm/18-in) fitted with a 1.7-cm/0.69-in plain tip (#809) with the choux paste. Pipe the paste into 5-cm/2-in mounds with 2.5-cm/1-in spacing on the baking mat or parchment paper. Brush the top with egg wash using a gentle dabbing motion.

2. Bake at 191°C/375°F for about 20 minutes until the choux are puffed up. Reduce the temperature to 177°C/350°F and bake for another 15 minutes until the choux are golden brown. Turn off the oven and leave the choux in the oven undisturbed for another 10 minutes. Remove the baked choux from the oven and let cool completely.

For 7.6-cm/3-in round large choux (makes about 12):

1. Preheat the oven to 191°C/375°F. Fill a large pastry bag (45.7-cm/18-in) fitted with a 1.7-cm/0.69-in plain tip (#809) with the choux paste. Pipe the paste into 6.4-cm/2.5-in mounds with 2.5-cm/1-in spacing on the baking mat or parchment paper. Brush the top with egg wash using a gentle dabbing motion.

2. Bake at 191°C/375°F for about 20 minutes until the choux are puffed up. Reduce the temperature to 177°C/350°F and bake for another 20 minutes until the choux are golden brown. Turn off the oven and leave the choux in the oven undisturbed for another 10 minutes. Remove the baked choux from the oven and let cool completely [22–24].

For 14-cm/5.5-in éclairs (makes about 14):

1. Preheat the oven to 191°C/375°F. Fill a large pastry bag (45.7-cm/18-in) fitted with a 1.3-cm/0.5-in fine star tip (#866) with the choux paste. Pipe the paste into 14-cm/5.5-in logs with 2.5-cm/1-in spacing on the baking mat or parchment paper [25, 26]. Brush the top with egg wash using a gentle dabbing motion [27].

2. Bake at 191°C/375°F for about 18 minutes until the éclairs are puffed up. Reduce the temperature to 177°C/350°F and bake for another 15 minutes until

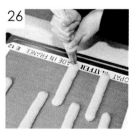

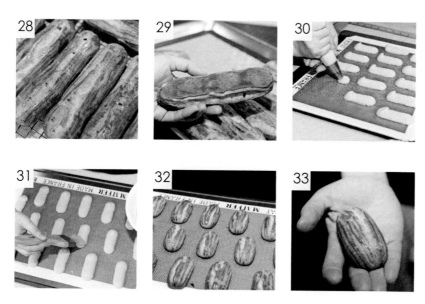

the éclairs are golden brown. Turn off the oven and leave the éclairs in the oven undisturbed for another 10 minutes. Remove the baked éclairs from the oven and let cool completely [28, 29].

For 6.4-cm/2.5-in mini éclairs (makes about 36):

1. Preheat the oven to 191°C/375°F. Fill a large pastry bag (45.7-cm/18-in) fitted with a 1.3-cm/0.5-in fine star tip (#866) with the choux paste. Pipe the paste into 6.4-cm/2.5-in logs with 2.5-cm/1-in spacing on the baking mat or parchment paper [30]. Brush the top with egg wash using a gentle dabbing motion [31].

2. Bake at 191°C/375°F for about 15 minutes until the éclairs are puffed up. Reduce the temperature to 177°C/350°F and bake for another 15 minutes until the éclairs are golden brown. Turn off the oven and leave the éclairs in the oven undisturbed for another 10 minutes. Remove the baked éclairs from the oven and let cool completely [32, 33].

CRUMBLE-COOKIE TOPPING

Nutty and crumbly, this cookie topping is the perfect addition to any choux creation. You can prepare the cookie dough ahead of time. When ready to use, simply roll out the dough and cut out the desired shapes and sizes. Be sure to keep the cookie cutouts chilled until just before baking.

Yield: about 200 g/7.1 oz crumble-cookie dough

INGREDIENTS

50 g/1.8 oz all-purpose flour

50 g/1.8 oz almond flour

50 g/1.8 oz light brown sugar

Pinch of kosher salt or fine sea salt

50 g/1.8 oz unsalted butter cubes, at room temperature

1. Combine the flour, almond flour, light brown sugar, and salt in a food processor [1].

2. Pulse the food processor a few times to evenly distribute the ingredients.

3. Add the soft butter pieces [2]. Pulse the machine a few more times until a smooth dough forms [3, 4]. Do not over-mix.

4. Place the dough between two pieces of plastic wrap and flatten the dough slightly [5, 6]. Chill for two hours in the refrigerator before using.

PASTRY CREAM

The simple technique and versatile applications make pastry cream an essential component in a pastry kitchen. Simply whip the pastry cream and use it by itself as a filling or use the pastry cream as the base for other creams.

Yield: about 580 g/20.5 oz pastry cream

INGREDIENTS

80 g/2.8 oz egg yolks

50 g/1.8 oz granulated sugar (A)

30 g/1.1 oz cornstarch

400 g/14.1 oz whole milk

50 g/1.8 oz granulated sugar (B)

1 vanilla bean

30 g/1.1 oz unsalted butter, at room temperature

1. Combine egg yolks, sugar (A), and cornstarch in a stainless steel mixing bowl. Mix well with a balloon whisk. Set aside [1, 2].

2. Place the milk and sugar (B) in a medium-sized stainless steel saucepan. Use a paring knife to split the vanilla bean lengthwise. Scrape off the vanilla seeds using the back of the knife [3]. Add the vanilla bean halves and seeds to the saucepan.

3. Heat the milk mixture over medium-high heat [4]. Remove from heat when it comes to a boil. Remove the vanilla bean halves. Pour about half of the hot liquid into the reserved egg yolk mixture while whisking vigorously [5]. Pour the mixture back into the pan [6]. Cook the mixture over medium-low heat while whisking constantly for 1 to 2 minutes until the mixture thickens [7]. Let cool slightly. Stir in the soft butter and mix well [8].

4. Cover the surface of the pastry cream with plastic wrap. Store in the refrigerator if not using immediately. Use at room temperature.

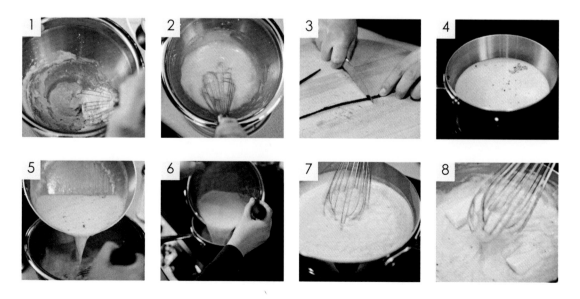

CHOCOLATE PASTRY CREAM

The method for making chocolate pastry cream is quite similar to the method for pastry cream with the exception of added dark chocolate. For best results, use high-quality chocolate couverture in the recipe.

Yield: about 530 g/18.7 oz chocolate pastry cream

INGREDIENTS

60 g/2.1 oz egg yolks

35 g/1.2 oz granulated sugar (A)

20 g/0.71 oz cornstarch

300 g/10.6 oz whole milk

35 g/1.2 oz granulated sugar (B)

1 vanilla bean

120 g/4.2 oz bittersweet dark chocolate couverture, finely chopped

60 g/2.1 oz unsalted butter, at room temperature

1. Combine egg yolks, sugar (A), and cornstarch in a stainless steel mixing bowl. Mix well with a balloon whisk [1]. Set aside.

2. Place the milk and sugar (B) in a medium-sized stainless steel saucepan. Use a paring knife to split the vanilla bean lengthwise. Scrape off the vanilla seeds using the back of the knife. Add the vanilla bean halves and seeds to the saucepan.

3. Heat the milk mixture over medium-high heat. Remove from heat when it comes to a boil. Remove the vanilla bean halves. Pour about half of the hot liquid into the reserved egg yolk mixture while whisking vigorously [2]. Pour the mixture back into the pan [3]. Cook the mixture over medium-low heat while whisking constantly for 1 to 2 minutes until the mixture thickens [4]. Remove from heat.

4. Stir in the dark chocolate pieces and mix well [5]. Stir in the soft butter and mix vigorously until the mixture is smooth and homogenous [6].

5. Cover the surface of the chocolate pastry cream with plastic wrap. Store in the refrigerator if not using immediately. Use at room temperature.

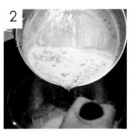
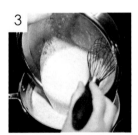
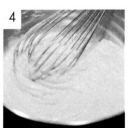

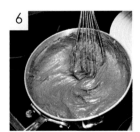

DIPPING CARAMEL

The traditional hard caramel topping adds the perfect crunch to profiteroles. This version of the dipping caramel produces a relatively light and transparent glaze, which is ideal for coloring. Be sure not to use too much glaze on the choux; if you do, the topping will be too hard to eat.

INGREDIENTS

500 g/17.6 oz granulated sugar

200 g/7.1 oz distilled water

100 g/3.5 oz glucose syrup

1. Combine the sugar and water in a medium-sized stainless steel saucepan. Heat the mixture over medium heat. Stir with a spatula constantly until the sugar is dissolved; skim off any impurities or foam that flow to the top.

2. When the sugar syrup comes to a boil, stir in the glucose syrup [1]. Bring the mixture back to a boil.

3. Insert a candy thermometer [2] and stop stirring. Increase the heat to medium-high. Continue to cook the sugar; brush down the sides of the pan with a pastry brush dipped in cold water to prevent sugar crystals from forming [3].

4. Cook the sugar until it reaches 160°C/320°F, about 15 to 20 minutes' cooking time. Remove from heat and use the caramel immediately.

CHOCOLATE GLAZE

This is my favorite chocolate glaze. It is not overly sweet and is full of cocoa flavor. The glaze also produces a beautiful mirror-like sheen on the pastry that is simply stunning. Be sure to make the glaze in advance since it requires time to rest.

Yield: about 600 g/21.2 oz chocolate glaze

INGREDIENTS

10 g/0.35 oz sheet gelatin (silver grade) or 8.4 g/0.3 oz powdered gelatin + 50.4 g/1.8 oz cold water

90 g/3.2 oz unsweetened, Dutch-processed cocoa powder

175 g/6.2 oz heavy whipping cream

250 g/8.8 oz granulated sugar

90 g/3.2 oz distilled water

1. In a medium-sized bowl, bloom the sheet gelatin in plenty of cold water. If using powdered gelatin, sprinkle the powder over 50.4 g/1.8 oz cold water in the bowl. Let the gelatin bloom for at least 10 minutes before using.

2. Meanwhile, sift the cocoa powder and set aside.

3. Combine the cream, sugar, and water in a large stainless steel saucepan. Bring the mixture to a boil over medium-high heat [1].

4. Reduce the heat to low and whisk in the sifted cocoa powder [2]. Whisk constantly and cook the mixture for 1 to 2 minutes [3]. Remove from heat and let cool slightly.

5. Meanwhile, squeeze excess water out of the bloomed sheet gelatin and add the gelatin to the mixture [4, 5]. If using powdered gelatin, add the entire contents to the mixture. Whisk to combine [6].

6. Transfer the chocolate glaze mixture to a medium-sized mixing bowl [7]. Use an immersion blender to blend the mixture until it is smooth and glossy [8].

7. Cover the surface of the chocolate glaze with plastic wrap. Chill in the refrigerator overnight before using.

8. Let the chocolate glaze return to room temperature (around 25°C/77°F) before using.

Note: You can warm the glaze in a microwave. Gently heat the glaze in the microwave in 10-second increments and stir the glaze after each heating. Take care not to over-heat the glaze.

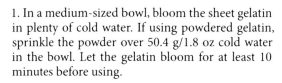

PASTRY FONDANT AND 30° BAUME SYRUP

Pastry fondant is one of the most commonly used glazes in a pastry kitchen. You can find ready-made pastry fondant from most pastry ingredient suppliers; however, it is well worth the effort to make your own. For best results, allow the fondant to rest overnight before using it; therefore, be sure to prepare it in advance if you plan to use homemade fondant in a recipe. For glazing applications, pastry fondant usually needs to be diluted with sugar syrup; 30° Baume syrup is often used for this purpose. The Baume scale is a standard measurement for liquid densities. The 30° Baume syrup contains approximately 55% sugar by weight at room temperature. Store any unused pastry fondant at room temperature in an airtight container or plastic wrap.

PASTRY FONDANT

Yield: about 600 g/21.2 oz pastry fondant

INGREDIENTS

500 g/17.6 oz granulated sugar

100 g/3.5 oz distilled water

100 g/3.5 oz glucose syrup

30° BAUME SYRUP

Yield: about 220 g/7.8 oz syrup

INGREDIENTS

120 g/4.2 oz granulated sugar

100 g/3.5 oz distilled water

PASTRY FONDANT

1. Combine the sugar and water in a medium-sized stainless steel saucepan. Heat the mixture over medium heat. Stir constantly with a spatula until the sugar is dissolved.

2. When the sugar syrup comes to a boil, stir in the glucose syrup [1]. Bring the mixture back to a boil.

3. Insert a candy thermometer [2] and stop stirring. Increase the heat to medium-high. Continue to cook the sugar; brush down the sides of the pan with a pastry brush dipped in cold water to prevent sugar crystals from forming [3].

4. Cook the sugar until it reaches 118°C/244°F. Let cool slightly. Pour the syrup into a food processor [4] and cover the food processor bowl tightly with plastic wrap.

5. Let the syrup cool to 80°C/176°F. Turn on the food processor. Mix until the syrup turns opaque, white, and glossy [5, 6].

6. Immediately transfer the white fondant into a container and cover its surface with plastic wrap. Let it rest at room temperature overnight. The fondant will become softer and more pliable.

30° BAUME SYRUP

In a medium-sized stainless steel saucepan, combine the sugar and water. Bring the mixture to a boil and remove from heat. Let the syrup cool completely before using. Store in an airtight container if not using immediately.

TART SHELLS

These tart shells are relatively easy to prepare and can be used in many pastry applications. You can make the dough or even the tart shells in advance. The baked tart shells can stay fresh for days at room temperature. Use them in choux tarts or any other of your favorite desserts.

Yield: about 580 g/20.5 oz tart dough; enough for 12 8-cm/3.1-in or 10 10-cm/3.9-in round tart shells

INGREDIENTS

250 g/8.8 oz all-purpose flour

30 g/1.1 oz almond flour

100 g/3.5 oz powdered sugar

1 g/0.035 oz (⅛ tsp) kosher salt or fine sea salt

1 vanilla bean

150 g/5.3 oz unsalted butter cubes, at room temperature

60 g/2.1 oz whole eggs, at room temperature

1. Combine the flour, almond flour, powdered sugar, and salt in a food processor. Pulse the machine a few times to evenly distribute all dry ingredients.

2. Use a paring knife to split the vanilla bean lengthwise. Scrape off the vanilla seeds using the back of the knife. Add the vanilla seeds and softened butter pieces to the food processor [1].

3. Pulse the machine a few more times until small pea-sized dough pieces are formed [2]. Add the whole eggs [3] and process for a few seconds until a smooth dough forms [4, 5]. Do not over-mix.

4. Wrap the dough between two pieces of plastic wrap and flatten the dough slightly [6, 7]. Chill in the refrigerator for about 2 hours.

5. Roll out the dough between two pieces of parchment paper to a 2-mm/0.08-in thickness [8]. Chill the dough again in the refrigerator for about 45 minutes or in the freezer for about 8 minutes.

6. Meanwhile, grease the inner rim of the tart rings with butter. Place the greased tart rings on a half-sheet pan lined with a half-sheet-sized silicone baking mat or parchment paper.

7. Remove the chilled dough from the refrigerator or freezer. Dock the dough with a dough docker or fork [9].

8. Using a paring knife, cut out circles that are roughly 12-cm/4.7-in in diameter for 8-cm/3.1-in tart rings or 14-cm/5.5-in in diameter for 10-cm/3.9-in tart rings [10].

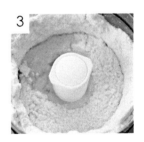

9. Place the dough disks on top of the tart rings. Gently press the dough into the tart rings. Use fingers to smooth the dough against the rings [11]. Use a knife to trim off excess dough on top of the rings [12, 13].

10. Place the lined tart shells and baking sheet in the refrigerator for another 30 minutes or in the freezer for 10 minutes.

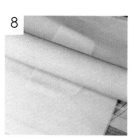

11. Meanwhile, preheat the oven to 177°C/350°F. Add parchment paper circles or baking cups in the center of lined tart shells. Press the parchment paper cups gently to fit inside the tart rings snugly [14]. Add beans or rice to the baking cups all the way to the top rim of the tart rings [15, 16].

12. Bake at 177°C/350°F for about 22 minutes for 8-cm/3.1-in tart shells or 27 minutes for 10-cm/3.9-in tart shells until they are light golden along the edges.

13. Let the tart shells cool slightly and then remove the baking cups filled with beans [17, 18]. Remove the tart shells from the tart rings [19]. Let cool completely before using.

14. Store in an airtight container if not used immediately.

INVERTED PUFF PASTRY DOUGH

Puff pastry contains hundreds of rich, buttery, crispy thin layers. The classic puff pastry dough consists of a butter block (beurrage) and a regular flour dough (détrempe). To produce hundreds of thin layers, a technique known as the lamination process is employed. The butter block is first encased in the flour dough, and then the dough is rolled out and folded several times to create hundreds of alternating layers of dough and butter. Similar to the classic puff pastry dough, the inverted puff pastry dough is also composed of two parts—a butter dough with butter as its primary ingredient and a regular dough with a small amount of butter. Unlike the classic puff pastry dough, to make the inverted puff pastry dough, the regular flour dough is encased in the butter dough, hence the name inverted puff pastry. The inverted puff pastry dough is much easier to roll out and it is more forgiving than its classic counterpart. The result is equally as impressive as the original version. Because the puff pastry dough freezes very well, you can store any leftover dough in the freezer for later use.

Yield: about 1.2 kg /2.64 lb puff pastry dough

INGREDIENTS

Dough A (Beurrage):

400 g/14.1 oz unsalted butter cubes, cold but pliable

175 g/6.2 oz all-purpose flour

Dough B (Détrempe):

350 g/12.3 oz all-purpose flour

175 g/6.2 oz distilled water

10 g/0.35 oz kosher salt or fine sea salt

100 g/3.5 oz unsalted butter, melted and cooled

Dough A (Beurrage):

1. Combine the butter cubes and flour for the beurrage in a mixer bowl. Attach the mixer bowl to the mixer fitted with a paddle attachment. Mix the ingredients at medium speed until a smooth dough forms [1, 2].

2. Place the dough between two pieces of plastic wrap. Shape the dough into a square [3, 4]. Chill the dough in the refrigerator for 30 minutes to an hour.

Dough B (Détrempe):

1. Combine the flour, water, salt, and melted butter for the détrempe in a mixer bowl. Attach the mixer bowl to the mixer fitted with a dough hook attachment. Mix the ingredients at medium speed until a smooth dough forms [5, 6].

2. Place the dough between two pieces of plastic wrap. Shape the dough into a square [7]. Chill the dough in the refrigerator for 30 minutes to an hour.

Lamination Process:

1. Roll out Dough B into a rectangle that is about 28-cm x 20-cm/11-in x 7.9-in in size and set aside [8].

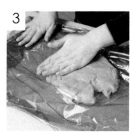

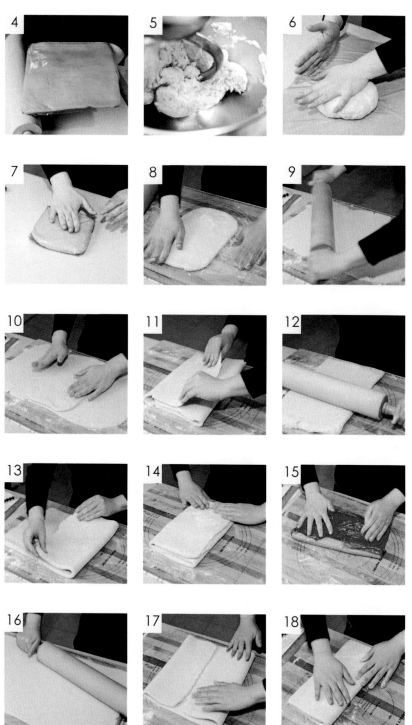

2. Roll out Dough A into a rectangle that is about 40-cm x 28-cm/15.7-in x 11-in in size [9].

3. Place Dough B in the center of Dough A so that the shorter sides of Dough B are flush with the longer sides of Dough A [10]. Wrap Dough A around Dough B to form a dough block that is about 28-cm x 20-cm/11-in x 7.9-in in size [11].

4. Roll out the dough block to about 40-cm x 28-cm/15.7-in x 11-in [12]. Give the laminated dough a single turn by folding the dough in thirds along its longer sides [13, 14], similar to folding a letter. Wrap the dough with plastic wrap [15] and chill for an hour.

5. Roll the dough out to about 40-cm x 28-cm/15.7-in x 11-in again [16]. Give the dough a double turn by folding the dough in fourths along its longer sides and close the dough [17, 18], similar to closing a book. Wrap the dough with plastic wrap and chill for an hour.

6. Repeat to give the dough another single turn, followed by a final double turn. Chill for an hour between turns.

7. Wrap the dough with plastic wrap and chill for an hour before using or store the dough in the refrigerator or freezer until ready to use.

CLASSIC

PROFITEROLES

Profiteroles are the most basic and traditional choux pastry to prepare. The possibilities for these delicious little bites are endless. In this recipe, we present five versions of the most popular topping options—pearl sugar, caramel, chocolate glaze, fondant glaze, and crumble-cookie. We use classic pastry creams as the fillings. Once you have mastered the techniques for creating these profiteroles, you can develop your own favorite toppings, fillings, and flavor combinations.

Yield: about 60 3.8-cm/1.5-in mini profiteroles for each topping option

INGREDIENTS

Profiteroles with Pearl Sugar:

1 recipe pâte à choux (page 12)

Pearl sugar

580 g/20.5 oz pastry cream (page 17)

Profiteroles with Caramel Topping:

1 recipe pâte à choux (page 12)

1 recipe dipping caramel (page 19)

580 g/20.5 oz pastry cream (page 17)

Profiteroles with Dark Chocolate Glaze:

600 g/21.2 oz chocolate glaze (page 20)

1 recipe pâte à choux (page 12)

530 g/18.7 oz chocolate pastry cream (page 18)

Profiteroles with Fondant Icing:

300 g/10.6 oz pastry fondant (page 21)

80 g/2.8 oz 30° Baume syrup (page 21)

1 recipe pâte à choux (page 12)

580 g/20.5 oz pastry cream (page 17)

Profiteroles with Pearl Sugar:

1. Follow the directions on page 12 to make round mini choux. Just before baking, sprinkle the pearl sugar granules on top of the piped choux paste [1]. Bake the choux according to the directions on page 13 [2].

2. When the baked choux are completely cooled, use a 0.8-cm/0.31-in fine star tip (#863) to punch a hole in the bottom of each chou [3, 4].

3. Follow the directions on page 17 to make the pastry cream. When the pastry cream is cooled completely, whisk it in a stand mixer until it is light and smooth.

4. Fill a large pastry bag (45.7-cm/18-in) fitted with a 0.6-cm/0.25-in plain tip (#802) with the whipped pastry cream. Pipe a small amount of pastry cream into each chou through the hole in the bottom [5]. Repeat until all of the choux are filled.

Profiteroles with Caramel Topping:

1. Follow the directions on page 12 to make round mini choux [6]. When the baked choux are completely cooled, use a 0.8-cm/0.31-in fine star tip (#863) to punch a hole in the bottom of each chou.

2. Follow the directions on page 19 to make the dipping caramel. When the caramel reaches the desired temperature, remove from heat. Allow the bubbles to subside slightly. Transfer the caramel to a heat-proof pitcher and then pour a small amount of caramel into the cavities of 4.1-cm/1.6-in half-sphere silicone molds to about ⅓ full [7].

Profiteroles with Crumble-Cookie Topping:

200 g/7.1 oz crumble-cookie topping (page 16)

1 recipe pâte à choux (page 12)

580 g/20.5 oz pastry cream (page 17)

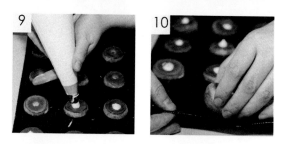

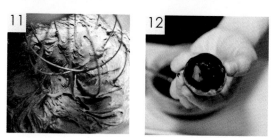

3. Quickly insert the choux into caramel-filled molds with the bottom-side up [8]. Let the caramel harden completely.

Note: If silicone molds are not available, you can dip the choux directly into the caramel and place the glazed choux on a silicone baking mat or a piece of parchment paper with the caramel-coated side down.

4. Meanwhile, follow the directions on page 17 to make the pastry cream. When the pastry cream is cooled completely, whisk it in a stand mixer until it is light and smooth.

5. Fill a large pastry bag (45.7-cm/18-in) fitted with a 0.6-cm/0.25-in plain tip (#802) with the pastry cream. Pipe a small amount of pastry cream into each chou through the hole in the bottom [9]. Carefully remove the filled choux from the silicone molds [10].

Profiteroles with Dark Chocolate Glaze:

1. On the day before baking, follow the directions on page 20 to make the chocolate glaze and allow the glaze to set overnight in the refrigerator.

2. On the day of baking, follow the directions on page 12 to make round mini choux. When the baked choux are completely cooled, use a 0.8-cm/0.31-in fine star tip (#863) to punch a hole in the bottom of each chou.

3. Follow the directions on page 18 to make the chocolate pastry cream. When the chocolate pastry cream is cooled completely, whisk it in a stand mixer until the cream is light and smooth [11].

4. Fill a large pastry bag (45.7-cm/18-in) fitted with a 0.6-cm/0.25-in plain tip (#802) with the chocolate pastry cream. Pipe a small amount of cream into each chou through the hole in the bottom.

5. Gently heat the chocolate glaze in a microwave at 10-second increments and stir the glaze after each heating. Take care not to over-heat the glaze. Use the glaze at 25°C/77°F.

6. Dip the filled chou into the chocolate glaze [12]. Gently shake off excess glaze and place the chou bottom-side down on a piece of parchment paper. Repeat until all the choux are glazed.

Profiteroles with Fondant Icing:

1. On the day before baking, follow the directions on page 21 to make the pastry fondant and 30° Baume syrup. Allow the fondant to set overnight at room temperature.

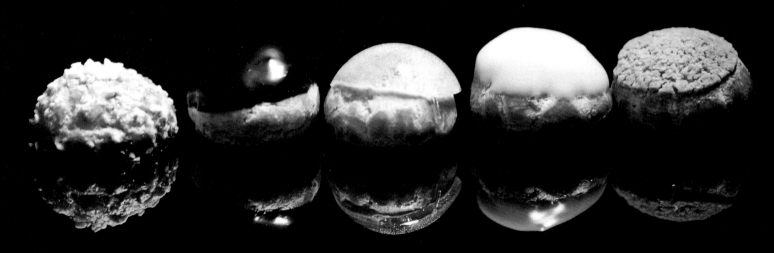

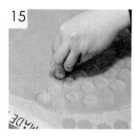

2. On the day of baking, follow the directions on page 12 to make round mini choux. When the baked choux are completely cooled, use a 0.8-cm/0.31-in fine star tip (#863) to punch a hole in the bottom of each chou.

3. Follow the directions on page 17 to make the pastry cream. When the pastry cream is cooled completely, whisk it in a stand mixer until it is light and smooth.

4. Fill a large pastry bag (45.7-cm/18-in) fitted with a 0.6-cm/0.25-in plain tip (#802) with the pastry cream. Pipe a small amount of cream into each chou through the hole in the bottom.

5. In a medium-sized mixing bowl, combine the pastry fondant and 30° Baume syrup. Gently heat the mixture over a double-boiler or in a microwave until the mixture reaches 37°C/99°F. Do not heat the mixture hotter than 50°C/122°F.

6. Dip the filled chou into the diluted pastry fondant [13, 14]. Gently shake off excess glaze and place the chou bottom-side down on a piece of parchment paper. Repeat until all the choux are glazed.

Profiteroles with Crumble-Cookie Topping:

1. Follow the directions on page 16 to make the crumble-cookie topping. Roll out the dough between two pieces of parchment paper to 2-mm/0.08-in thick. Chill the dough in the refrigerator for about 45 minutes or in the freezer for about 10 minutes.

2. Remove the chilled dough from the refrigerator or freezer. Use a 2.2-cm/0.9-in round pastry cutter to cut out circular disks from the dough [15]. Return the cookie disks to the refrigerator or freezer until ready to use.

3. Follow the directions on page 12 to make round mini choux. Just before baking, place the crumble-cookie disks on top of the piped choux paste [16]. Bake the choux according to the directions on page 13. When the baked choux are completely cooled, use a 0.8-cm/0.31-in fine star tip (#863) to punch a hole in the bottom of each chou.

4. Follow the directions on page 17 to make the pastry cream. When the pastry cream is cooled completely, whisk it in a stand mixer until it is light and smooth.

5. Fill a large pastry bag (45.7-cm/18-in) fitted with a 0.6-cm/0.25-in plain tip (#802) with the pastry cream. Pipe a small amount of cream into each chou through the hole in the bottom. Repeat until all the choux are filled.

CREAM PUFFS

Delicious choux filled with vanilla Chantilly cream, slightly crispy on the outside and light as a cloud, the classic cream puff never goes out of style. Although it has only a handful of ingredients, when properly made, this simple dessert will impress even the most refined palate.

Yield: about 18 cream puffs

INGREDIENTS

Medium-Sized Choux:

1 recipe pâte à choux (page 12)

Chantilly Cream:

500 g/17.6 oz heavy whipping cream

70 g/2.5 oz granulated sugar

1 vanilla bean

Assembly and Decoration:

Powdered sugar for dusting

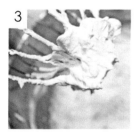

Medium-Sized Choux:

Follow the directions on page 12 to make round medium-sized choux.

Chantilly Cream:

1. In a mixer bowl, combine the chilled heavy cream and sugar. Use a paring knife to split the vanilla bean lengthwise. Scrape off the vanilla seeds using the back of the knife [1]. Add the vanilla seeds to the mixture.

2. Attach the mixer bowl to a mixer fitted with a whisk attachment. Whisk the mixture on medium speed until the cream thickens slightly [2]. Increase the speed to high and whisk the cream until stiff peaks form [3]. Do not over-beat.

Assembly and Decoration:

1. Using a serrated knife, cut off the top ⅓ of each chou [4] and reserve the cap.

2. Fill a large pastry bag (45.7-cm/18-in) fitted with a 1-cm/0.38-in fine star tip (#864) with the Chantilly cream.

3. Pipe the cream into the bottom portion of the chou [5]. Place the reserved cap on top of the cream [6, 7]. Dust the top with powdered sugar if desired [8].

CHOCOLATE ÉCLAIRS

The classic éclair has regained its popularity in today's fast-evolving pastry scene. While contemporary éclair creations come in a wide range of colors, forms, and flavors, the traditional chocolate éclair still hasn't lost its charm. Airy and crispy choux filled with tantalizing chocolate cream and covered with a thin layer of mirror glaze of dark chocolate coating. No wonder it is still as irresistible as ever.

Yield: about 14 14-cm/5.5-in éclairs

INGREDIENTS

Éclairs:

1 recipe pâte à choux (page 12)

Chocolate Filling:

530 g/18.7 oz chocolate pastry cream (page 18)

Assembly and Decoration:

600 g/21.2 oz chocolate glaze (page 20)

Edible gold leaves (optional)

Éclairs:

1. Follow the directions on page 12 to make the 14-cm/5.5-in éclairs [1].

2. When the baked éclairs are completely cooled, use a 1-cm/0.38-in fine star tip (#864) to punch three holes in the bottom of each éclair [2].

Chocolate Filling:

Follow the directions on page 18 to make the chocolate pastry cream. When the chocolate pastry cream is cooled completely, whisk it in a stand mixer until it is light and smooth [3].

Assembly and Decoration:

1. Fill a large pastry bag (45.7-cm/18-in) fitted with a 0.8-cm/0.31-in plain tip (#803) with the chocolate pastry cream. Pipe the cream into each éclair through the holes in the bottom [4].

2. Gently heat the chocolate glaze (page 20) in a microwave at 10-second increments and stir the glaze after each heating. Take care not to over-heat the glaze. Use the glaze at 25°C/77°F.

3. Dip the filled éclair into the chocolate glaze [5, 6]. Gently shake off excess glaze and place the éclair bottom-side down on a piece of parchment paper or cooling rack. Repeat until all the éclairs arc glazed.

4. Decorate the top of the éclairs with edible gold leaves if desired [7, 8].

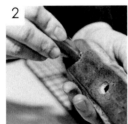

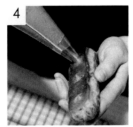

PARIS-BREST

This beloved French classic was created to commemorate the bicycle race from Paris to Brest. Although there are numerous variations, the classic version has the ring-shaped choux pastries filled with hazelnut praline cream; it is usually topped with sliced almonds and dusted with powdered sugar.

Yield: about 10 9-cm/3.5-in ring-shaped choux pastries

INGREDIENTS

Choux Rings:

1 recipe pâte à choux (page 12)

Powdered sugar for dusting

Sliced almonds

Hazelnut Mousseline Cream:

550 g/19.4 oz pastry cream (page 17)

200 g/7.1 oz hazelnut paste

320 g/11.3 oz unsalted butter, at room temperature

Assembly and Decoration:

Powdered sugar for dusting

Choux Rings:

1. Preheat the oven to 191°C/375°F. Follow the directions on page 12 to make the choux paste.

2. Line a baking pan with a silicone baking mat or parchment paper. Dust the baking surface with powdered sugar [1]; use a 7-cm/2.8-in round pastry cutter to make round impressions in the dusted sugar [2].

3. Fill a large pastry bag (45.7-cm/18-in) fitted with a 1.4-cm/0.56-in fine star tip (#867) with the choux paste; pipe the paste along the circular outline in the dusted sugar to make a ring. Repeat to pipe more choux rings [3].

4. Gently brush the choux rings with egg wash [4]. Sprinkle sliced almonds on top [5].

5. Bake at 191°C/375°F for 16 to 18 minutes until the choux rings are puffed up. Reduce the temperature to 177°C/350°F and bake for another 15 minutes until the choux rings are golden brown. Turn off the oven and leave the choux rings in the oven undisturbed for another 10 minutes. Remove the baked choux rings from the oven and let cool completely [6].

Hazelnut Mousseline Cream:

1. Combine the pastry cream (page 17) with hazelnut paste in a mixer bowl. Beat with a stand mixer fitted with a wire whisk attachment on medium-high speed until the mixture is smooth.

2. Reduce the mixer speed to medium-low and whisk in the soft butter in small increments [7]. Make sure each addition of butter is thoroughly incorporated before adding more. Scrape down the sides of the bowl with a spatula if necessary.

3. Once all the butter is incorporated, adjust the mixer to medium-high speed. Continue to beat for a few more minutes until the cream is light and fluffy [8].

Assembly and Decoration:

1. Using a serrated knife, cut each ring in half horizontally [9]. Reserve the top portion.

2. Fill a large pastry bag (45.7-cm/18-in) fitted with a 1-cm/0.38-in fine star tip (#864) with the hazelnut mousseline cream. Pipe the cream on the bottom half of each ring in a circular motion [10–12].

3. Place the top half of ring on top of the cream and dust the top with powdered sugar [13, 14]. Repeat to assemble more pastries.

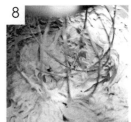

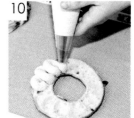

CARAMEL ÉCLAIRS

Another timeless classic that will satisfy any sweet tooth, these little sinfully delicious treats filled with salted butter caramel cream are absolutely addictive!

Yield: about 36 6.4-cm/2.5-in mini éclairs

INGREDIENTS

Mini Éclairs:

1 recipe pâte à choux (page 12)

Salted Caramel:

200 g/7.1 oz heavy whipping cream

125 g/4.4 oz granulated sugar

2.5 g/0.088 oz (⅓ tsp) kosher salt or fine sea salt

Caramel Mousseline Cream:

220 g/7.8 oz pastry cream (page 17)

220 g/7.8 oz salted caramel (see above)

100 g/3.5 oz unsalted butter, at room temperature

Assembly and Decoration:

300 g/10.6 oz pastry fondant (page 21)

30 g/1.1 oz salted caramel (see above)

50 g/1.8 oz 30° Baume syrup (page 21)

Caramel coloring (optional)

Mini Éclairs:

1. Follow the directions on page 12 to make the 6.4-cm/2.5-in mini éclairs [1].

2. When the baked éclairs are completely cooled, use a 1-cm/0.38-in fine star tip (#864) to punch a hole in the bottom of each éclair [2].

Salted Caramel:

1. To make the caramel, place the heavy cream in a medium-sized stainless steel saucepan and set aside.

2. Place the sugar in a large stainless steel saucepan in an even layer. Dry melt the sugar over medium heat undisturbed for 3 to 5 minutes [3].

3. Meanwhile, heat the cream over high heat. Remove the pan from heat when the cream comes to a boil. Reserve.

4. When most of the sugar underneath the top layer of granules is melted and has turned a golden color, reduce the heat to low. Stir occasionally with a spatula to avoid burning the caramel [4].

5. When all of the sugar is melted and the caramel turns medium-dark amber at around 180°C/356°F, pour the hot cream into the pan [5]. Stir vigorously to smooth out any lumps [6].

6. Continue to cook the caramel for another 2 to 3 minutes while stirring constantly. Cook until the caramel is smooth and velvety. Remove from heat, add salt [7], and stir to combine.

7. Let the caramel cool slightly. Cover the surface of the caramel with plastic wrap. Allow the caramel to cool completely.

Caramel Mousseline Cream:

Combine the pastry cream (page 17) and 220 g/7.8 oz salted caramel in a mixer bowl [8]. Reserve the remaining caramel for the glaze. Attach the bowl to a stand mixer fitted with a whisk attachment. Whisk the mixture on medium-high speed until it is smooth and creamy. Add the soft butter [9]. Whisk again on high speed for a few minutes until the caramel cream is smooth and light [10].

Assembly and Decoration:

1. Fill a large pastry bag (45.7-cm/18-in) fitted with a 0.8-cm/0.31-in plain tip (#803) with the caramel mousseline cream. Pipe the cream into each éclair through the hole in the bottom [11].

2. To make the caramel fondant glaze, in a medium-sized mixing bowl, combine the pastry fondant, 30 g/1.1 oz of the reserved caramel, and 30° Baume syrup [12]. Add a small amount of brown gel coloring into the mixture if desired. Gently heat the mixture over a double-boiler or in a microwave until the mixture reaches 37°C/99°F. Do not heat the mixture hotter than 50°C/122°F.

3. Dip the filled éclair into the caramel fondant glaze [13]. Gently shake off excess glaze and place the éclair bottom-side down on a piece of parchment paper. Repeat until all the éclairs are glazed [14].

DOUGHNUTS

Made from choux paste, these doughnuts are airy, light, and absolutely heavenly. Simply dust them with cinnamon sugar or fill the interior with your favorite cream; either way, you will fall in love with these little morsels of goodness.

Yield: about 30 5-cm/2-in round doughnuts

INGREDIENTS

1 recipe pâte à choux (page 12)

Oil for frying

200 g/7.1 oz granulated sugar

2 g/0.071 oz (1 tsp) cinnamon powder

1. Follow the directions on page 12 to make the choux paste. Cover the surface of the choux paste with plastic wrap. Chill the paste in the refrigerator for about an hour.

2. Heat the oil in a Dutch oven or deep fryer to 185°C/365°F.

3. Remove the chilled choux paste from the refrigerator. Use a 3.8-cm/1.5-in ice cream scoop, preferably with a spring action release, to scoop up the choux paste and carefully drop it into the hot oil [1].

4. Fry the doughnuts for 10 to 12 minutes until they are golden brown and puffed up. Turn the doughnuts over half way during cooking [2].

5. Remove the doughnuts from the hot oil. Drain excess oil on paper towels [3].

6. In a medium-sized mixing bowl, combine the sugar and cinnamon powder. Coat the doughnuts in the cinnamon sugar [4]. Serve immediately.

RELIGIEUSES

Religieuse, or nun in French, is a pastry made from two filled choux with the slightly larger chou on the bottom. The pastry is named for its resemblance to the silhouette of a nun in habit. Although many versions of the pastry exist, this version has the classic dark chocolate glaze, light vanilla cream filling, and piping decoration that embraces the smaller chou. Eating this simple yet delightful pastry is a religious experience in the most delicious sense.

Yield: about 10 to 12 individual pastries

Ingredients

Mini and Large Choux:

1 recipe pâte à choux (page 12)

Vanilla Mousseline Cream:

550 g/19.4 oz pastry cream (page 17)

200 g/7.1 oz unsalted butter, at room temperature

Assembly and Decoration:

600 g/21.2 oz chocolate glaze (page 20)

White chocolate pearls or sugar pearls

Mini and Large Choux:

1. Follow the directions on page 12 to make the choux paste. Use ⅓ of the paste to make round mini choux and use the remaining ⅔ of the paste to make round large choux. Bake the choux according to the directions on pages 13 to 14 for mini and large choux [1–3].

2. When the baked choux are completely cooled, use a 1-cm/0.38-in fine star tip (#864) to punch a hole in the bottom of each chou [4–6].

Vanilla Mousseline Cream:

1. Place the pastry cream (page 17) in a mixer bowl. Beat with a stand mixer fitted with a wire whisk attachment on medium-high speed until the cream is smooth.

2. Reduce the mixer speed to medium-low and whisk in the soft butter in small increments. Make sure each addition of butter is thoroughly incorporated before adding more. Scrape down the sides of the bowl with a spatula if necessary.

3. Once all the butter is incorporated, adjust the mixer speed to medium-high. Continue to beat for a few more minutes until the cream is light and fluffy [7].

Assembly and Decoration:

1. Fill a large pastry bag (45.7-cm/18-in) fitted with a 0.8-cm/0.31-in plain tip (#803) with ¾ of the vanilla mousseline cream. Pipe the cream into each chou through the hole in the bottom [8, 9].

2. Gently heat the chocolate glaze (page 20) in a microwave at 10-second increments and stir the glaze after each heating. Take care not to overheat the glaze. Use the glaze at 25°C/77°F.

3. Dip the filled chou into the chocolate glaze [10, 11]. Gently shake off excess glaze and place the chou bottom-side down on a piece of parchment paper. Repeat until all of the choux are glazed.

4. Place the filled and glazed mini choux on top of the large choux.

5. Fill a medium-sized pastry bag (30.5-cm/12-in) fitted with a 0.4-cm/0.16-in closed star tip (#840) with the remaining vanilla mousseline cream. Pipe dollops of cream along the bottom edge of the mini choux in an upward direction [12, 13].

6. Decorate the top of the mini choux with white chocolate or sugar pearls if desired [14].

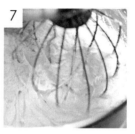

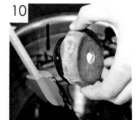

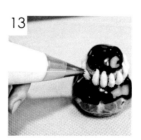

SAINT-HONORÉS

Named after the French patron saint of bakers and created by pastry chef Chiboust in Paris around the mid-nineteenth century, this classic masterpiece is a true test for any skillful pastry chef. It has a buttery, flaky puff pastry base that is topped with caramel glazed choux. Traditionally, the pastry is filled with Chiboust cream. Named after its creator, Chiboust cream contains a combination of pastry cream and meringue. The cream is piped using a special piping tip called a St. Honoré tip. The modern version of this pastry sometimes replaces the Chiboust cream with diplomat cream. In addition to the traditional cake version, the modern St. Honoré also has a smaller variation in individual serving sizes. Although St. Honoré is a relatively complicated pastry to produce, I think it is well worth the effort. This pastry always reminds me of why I love pastries so much in the first place.

Yield: 1 24-cm/9.4-in St. Honoré cake or 6 8-cm/3.1-in individual St. Honoré pastries

INGREDIENTS

Mini Choux and Cake Base:

1 recipe pâte à choux (page 12)

400 g/14.1 oz puff pastry dough (page 24)

Diplomat Cream:

550 g/19.4 oz pastry cream (page 17)

275 g/9.7 oz heavy whipping cream

Assembly and Decoration:

1 recipe dipping caramel (page 19)

Mini Choux and Cake Base:

1. Preheat the oven to 191°C/375°F. Follow the directions on page 12 to make the choux paste. Use ½ the choux paste to make about 30 round mini choux [1]. Reserve the remaining choux paste for the cake base.

2. When the baked choux are completely cooled, use a 0.8-cm/0.31-in fine star tip (#863) to punch a hole in the bottom of each chou [2].

3. Meanwhile, roll out the puff pastry dough (page 24) to about 3-mm/0.1-in thick [3]. Dock the dough with a dough docker or fork [4]. Cut out a 24-cm/9.4-in circle using a 24-cm/9.4-in tart ring as a guide [5]. Since the puff pastry dough will shrink a little during baking, cut along the outer edge of the tart ring.

4. Butter the inner rim of the tart ring and place it on a baking pan lined with parchment paper or a silicone mat. Place the puff pastry disk inside the tart ring.

5. Pipe the choux paste along the inside edge of the tart ring on top of the puff pastry disk [6]. Pipe another smaller circle of choux paste, about 10-cm/3.9-in in diameter, in the center of the puff pastry disk [7].

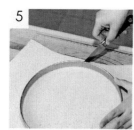

6. Loosely cover the top of the tart ring with plastic wrap [8] and place the baking pan in the refrigerator for 30 minutes to an hour.

7. Preheat the oven to 177°C/350°F. Remove the baking pan from the refrigerator. Lightly brush the top of the puff pastry-choux cake base with egg wash. Bake the cake base for about 40 to 45 minutes until it turns golden brown. Let cool completely before assembling the cake.

Diplomat Cream:

1. Place the pastry cream (page 17) in a mixer bowl. Attach the bowl to a stand mixer fitted with a whisk attachment. Whisk the pastry cream until it is light and creamy.

2. Whip the chilled heavy cream to stiff peaks by hand or using a mixer. Fold about ⅓ of the whipped cream into the pastry cream using a spatula. Mix until the mixture is homogenous. Gently fold in the remaining ⅔ of the whipped cream [9].

3. Reserve the diplomat cream in the refrigerator until ready to use.

Assembly and Decoration:

1. Follow the directions on page 19 to make the dipping caramel. When the caramel reaches the desired temperature, remove from heat. Allow the bubbles to subside slightly. Transfer the caramel into a heat-proof pitcher and then pour a small amount of caramel into the cavities of 4.1-cm/1.6-in half-sphere silicone molds to about ⅓ full [10].

2. Quickly insert the choux into caramel-filled molds with the bottom-side up [11]. Let the caramel harden completely before continuing.

Note: If silicone molds are not available, you can dip the choux directly into the caramel and place the glazed choux on a silicone baking mat or a piece of parchment paper with the caramel-coated side down.

3. Fill a large pastry bag (45.7-cm/18-in) fitted with a 0.6-cm/0.25-in plain tip (#802) with about ⅓ of the reserved diplomat cream. Pipe a small amount of the cream into each chou through the hole in the bottom [12].

4. Fill the center of the reserved puff pastry-choux cake base with diplomat cream. Use a large offset spatula to level the cream [13].

5. Carefully remove the filled choux from the silicone molds [14, 15]. Arrange about 10 to 12 filled mini choux along the outer edge of the cake base [16]. Leave about a 1.3-cm/0.5-in spacing between adjacent choux if desired.

6. Fill another large pastry bag (45.7-cm/18-in) fitted with a medium-sized St. Honoré tip (3-cm/1.2-in opening) with the remaining diplomat cream.

7. Pipe the cream between adjacent mini choux on the outer edge [17]. Pipe more cream in the center of the cake [18, 19]. If desired, alternate the piping angle of each stroke to achieve the traditional St. Honoré design.

Variation: Individual St. Honoré Pastries

1. For the puff pastry-choux cake bases [20–23], follow the directions for making the large cake base with these exceptions: Cut the puff pastry dough into 8-cm/3.1-in circles using an 8-cm/3.1-in tart ring, omit piping the small circle of choux paste in the center of puff pastry disk, and reduce the baking time to 30 to 35 minutes.

2. For assembly, fill the center of the puff pastry-choux bases with diplomat cream [24]. Arrange three mini choux on top [25].

3. Fill a large pastry bag (45.7-cm/18-in) fitted with a 1.3-cm/0.5-in closed star tip (#846) with the remaining diplomat cream. Pipe some cream between adjacent mini choux and on top of the choux [26, 27]. Finally, place another mini chou on top of the cream if desired [28].

3

CONTEMPORARY

RASPBERRY AND LYCHEE MASCARPONE

A playful reinvention of the raspberry and lychee duo, this time it is metamorphosed into a lovely "open-face" éclair. The airy and perfumed lychee mascarpone cream is accented with the refreshing raspberry-ginger jam. It is a sublime dessert that I absolutely adore!

Yield: about 14 14-cm/5.5-in éclairs

INGREDIENTS

Lychee Mascarpone Cream:

4 g/0.14 oz gelatin sheet (silver grade) or 3.4 g/0.12 oz powdered gelatin + 20.4 g/0.72 oz cold water

150 g/5.3 oz lychee puree

20 g/0.71 oz granulated sugar

100 g/3.5 oz mascarpone cheese, at room temperature

200 g/7.1 oz heavy whipping cream

Raspberry and Ginger Jam:

100 g/3.5 oz granulated sugar

4 g/0.14 oz (1 tsp) powdered pectin NH

200 g/7.1 oz raspberry puree

50 g/1.8 oz glucose syrup

3 g/0.11 oz (½ tsp) freshly grated ginger

Éclairs:

1 recipe pâte à choux (page 12)

Assembly and Decoration:

Fresh raspberries

Lychee Mascarpone Cream:

1. In a medium-sized bowl, bloom the sheet gelatin in plenty of cold water. If powdered gelatin is used, sprinkle the powder over 20.4 g/0.72 oz cold water in the bowl. Let the gelatin bloom for at least 10 minutes before using.

2. Combine the lychee puree and sugar in a medium-sized stainless steel saucepan. Mix well with a balloon whisk. Bring the mixture to 71°C/160°F over medium-high heat. Let cool slightly.

3. Meanwhile, squeeze excess water out of the bloomed sheet gelatin and add the gelatin to the lychee mixture [1]. If powdered gelatin is used, add the entire contents to the lychee mixture. Stir to combine. Cover the surface of the lychee jelly with plastic wrap. Let cool completely.

4. In a stand mixer fitted with a whisk attachment, whisk the mascarpone cheese until smooth. Gradually add the lychee jelly and whisk until the mixture is smooth and homogenous [2, 3]. Stir in the heavy cream with a spatula, but do not whisk. Chill the lychee mascarpone mixture in the refrigerator for 30 minutes to an hour.

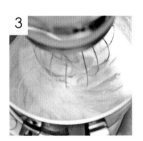

5. In a stand mixer fitted with a whisk attachment, whisk the chilled lychee mascarpone mixture until stiff peaks form [4]. Reserve the cream in the refrigerator until ready to use.

Raspberry and Ginger Jam:

1. Combine the sugar and pectin in a mixing bowl. Mix thoroughly and reserve.

2. In a medium-sized stainless steel saucepan, combine the raspberry puree, glucose syrup, and grated ginger [5]. Bring the mixture to a boil over medium-high heat. Stir in the sugar-pectin mixture [6]. Bring the mixture back to a boil and reduce the heat to medium-low. Stir constantly and cook for another five minutes.

3. Let cool slightly. Cover the surface of the raspberry-ginger jam with plastic wrap. Allow the jam to cool completely before using.

Éclairs:

Follow the directions on page 12 to make the 14-cm/5.5-in éclairs.

Assembly and Decoration:

1. Using a serrated knife, cut off the top half of each éclair horizontally [7].

2. Fill a medium-sized pastry bag (30.5-cm/12-in) fitted with a 0.6-cm/0.25-in plain tip (#802) with the raspberry and ginger jam. Pipe a small amount of the jam on the bottom of each éclair [8].

3. Add the lychee mascarpone cream on top of the jam. Use a small offset spatula to level the cream [9, 10].

4. Fill the cavities of fresh raspberries with the raspberry and ginger jam [11]. Place 4 to 5 filled raspberries on top of the lychee cream with the jam-filled side up [12].

5. Fill a large pastry bag (45.7-cm/18-in) fitted with a 0.8-cm/0.31-in closed star tip (#843) with the remaining lychee mascarpone cream. Pipe the cream into small rosettes on top of the éclair and around the raspberries [13, 14].

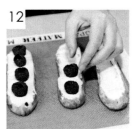

ESPRESSO AND CHOCOLATE

A reinterpretation of the classic pairing of coffee and chocolate, these whimsically shaped choux are filled with espresso-infused chocolate ganache cream that has been whipped to perfection and then topped with crunchy chocolate pearls. This is a simple yet elegant pastry creation that will satisfy the most discerning java 'n cocoa connoisseurs.

Yield: about 12 individual pastries

Ingredients

Espresso and Chocolate Cream:

860 g/30.3 oz heavy whipping cream

30 g/1.1 oz freshly ground espresso coffee beans

80 g/2.8 oz milk chocolate couverture, finely chopped

200 g/7.1 oz bittersweet dark chocolate couverture, finely chopped

Choux Base:

1 recipe pâte à choux (page 12)

Powdered sugar for dusting

Assembly and Decoration:

Crunchy white and dark chocolate pearls

Espresso and Chocolate Cream:

1. Combine the cream and ground coffee beans in a medium-sized stainless steel saucepan [1]. Bring the mixture to a boil. Remove from heat. Cover the pan and allow the mixture to infuse for about 15 minutes.

2. Meanwhile, place the milk and dark chocolates in a mixing bowl. Gently melt the chocolates using a double-boiler. Stir occasionally to allow even heating. Remove the chocolates from the double-boiler when about 75% of the chocolates is melted [2]. Reserve.

3. Bring the infused cream back to a boil and strain over the melted chocolates using a fine mesh strainer [3]. Wait 30 seconds and then stir the mixture until it is velvety smooth [4].

4. Cover the surface of the soft ganache cream with plastic wrap. Allow the ganache cream to set in the refrigerator overnight.

Choux Base:

1. Preheat the oven to 191°C/375°F. Follow the directions on page 12 to make the choux paste.

2. Line a baking pan with a silicone baking mat or parchment paper. Dust the baking surface with powdered sugar; use a 7-cm/2.8-in round pastry cutter to make round impressions in the dusted sugar [5].

3. Fill a large pastry bag (45.7-cm/18-in) fitted with a 1.4-cm/0.56-in fine star tip (#867) with the choux paste; pipe the paste along the circular outline in the dusted sugar to make a partial ring. Repeat to pipe more partial rings [6].

4. Gently brush the piped choux paste with egg wash [7]. Bake at 191°C/375°F for about 16 minutes until the choux rings are puffed up. Reduce the temperature to 177°C/350°F and bake for another 13 minutes until the choux rings are golden brown. Turn off the oven and leave the choux rings in the oven undisturbed for another 10 minutes. Remove the baked choux from the oven and let cool completely before continuing.

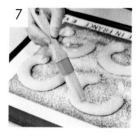

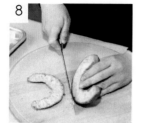

Assembly and Decoration:

1. Using a serrated knife, cut off the top ⅓ of each partial ring horizontally [8].

2. Transfer the chilled espresso and chocolate cream into a mixer bowl. Attach the bowl to a stand mixer fitted with a whisk attachment. Whisk the soft ganache cream on high speed until stiff peaks form [9].

3. Fill the bottom of each partial ring with the whipped espresso and chocolate cream. Use a small offset spatula to level the top [10].

4. Fill a large pastry bag (45.7-cm/18-in) fitted with a small St. Honoré tip (2-cm/0.8-in opening) with the remaining cream.

5. Pipe the espresso and chocolate cream along the contour of the partial ring while alternating the piping angle of each stroke [11, 12]. Sprinkle crunchy chocolate pearls on top if desired [13]. Repeat to assemble more pastries [14].

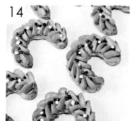

CALAMANSI AND BLACKBERRY

Calamansi is a popular citrus fruit in Southeast Asian that resembles a lime, but has a more acidic taste and fragrant aroma. In this delicate dessert, the unique flavor of calamansi is well balanced with mild blackberry cream and sweet, airy Italian meringue. If calamansi is not available, you can substitute lemon or lime puree.

Yield: 12 7.6-cm/3-in round choux pastries

Ingredients

Blackberry Cream:

2.5 g/0.088 oz gelatin sheet (silver grade) or 2.1 g/0.074 oz powdered gelatin + 12.6 g/0.44 oz cold water

230 g/8.1 oz blackberry puree

40 g/1.4 oz granulated sugar

15 g/0.53 oz cornstarch

Calamansi Cream:

6 g/0.21 oz gelatin sheet (silver grade) or 5 g/0.18 oz powdered gelatin + 30 g/1.1 oz cold water

220 g/7.8 oz whole eggs

150 g/5.3 oz granulated sugar

170 g/6 oz calamansi puree

180 g/6.3 oz unsalted butter, at room temperature

Large Choux:

1 recipe pâte à choux (page 12)

Italian Meringue:

120 g/4.2 oz egg whites

Blackberry Cream:

1. In a medium-sized bowl, bloom the sheet gelatin in plenty of cold water. If powdered gelatin is used, sprinkle the powder over 12.6 g/0.44 oz cold water in the bowl. Let the gelatin bloom for at least 10 minutes before using.

2. Combine the blackberry puree, sugar, and cornstarch in a medium-sized stainless steel saucepan. Mix well with a balloon whisk. Bring the mixture to a boil over medium-high heat while whisking constantly. Remove from heat when the mixture thickens. Let cool slightly.

3. Meanwhile, squeeze excess water out of the bloomed sheet gelatin and add the gelatin to the blackberry mixture [1]. If powdered gelatin is used, add the entire contents to the blackberry mixture. Stir to combine. Cover the surface of the blackberry cream with plastic wrap. Let cool completely.

4. Fill a large pastry bag (45.7-cm/18-in) fitted with a 1-cm/0.38-in plain tip (#804) with the blackberry cream. Pipe the cream into the cavities of 3-cm/1.2-in half-sphere silicone molds [2]. Place the filled molds in the freezer until ready to use.

Note: The silicone molds keep the blackberry cream filling in perfect dome shape, which makes an impressive presentation in the finished desserts. You can omit this step if silicone molds are not available.

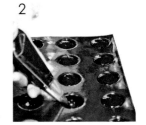

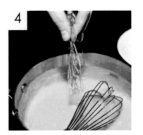

240 g/8.5 oz granulated sugar

60 g/2.1 oz distilled water

Assembly and Decoration:

Propane torch

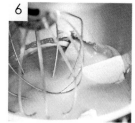

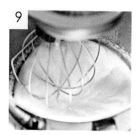

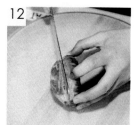

Calamansi Cream:

1. In a medium-sized bowl, bloom the sheet gelatin in plenty of cold water. If powdered gelatin is used, sprinkle the powder over 30 g/1.1 oz cold water in the bowl. Let the gelatin bloom for at least 10 minutes before using.

2. Combine eggs, sugar, and the calamansi puree in a medium-sized stainless steel saucepan. Heat the mixture over medium heat.

3. Whisk the mixture constantly to allow even heating [3]. Cook the mixture to 85°C/185°F and remove the pan from the heat. Take care not to over-heat the mixture; otherwise, the eggs in the mixture will coagulate. Let cool slightly.

4. Meanwhile, squeeze excess water out of the bloomed sheet gelatin and add the gelatin to the calamansi mixture [4]. If powdered gelatin is used, add the entire contents to the calamansi mixture. Stir to combine.

5. Pass the mixture through a fine mesh strainer [5]. Cover the surface of the calamansi mixture with plastic wrap. Let cool completely.

6. Combine the calamansi mixture and softened butter in a mixer bowl [6]. Attach the bowl to a stand mixer fitted with a whisk attachment. Whisk until the cream is light and smooth [7]. Allow the cream to set in the refrigerator for 2 hours before using.

Large Choux:

Follow the directions on page 12 to make the 7.6-cm/3-in round large choux.

Italian Meringue:

1. Place the egg whites in a mixer bowl and attach the bowl to a mixer fitted with the whisk attachment.

2. Cook the sugar and water in a saucepan over medium-high heat. Stir constantly until the sugar has dissolved. When the mixture comes to a boil, insert a candy thermometer and stop stirring [8]. When the sugar syrup reaches 110°C/230°F, turn on the mixer and start to beat the egg whites at high speed [9].

3. When the sugar syrup reaches 118°C/244°F, remove the saucepan from the heat. Slowly pour the syrup in a steady stream along the sides of the mixer bowl while the mixer is whisking [10]. Continue to beat until medium-soft peaks form [11] and the meringue has cooled to about 47°C/117°F.

Assembly and Decoration:

1. Using a serrated knife, cut off the top ⅓ of each chou [12].

2. Fill a large pastry bag (45.7-cm/18-in) fitted with a 1-cm/0.38-in plain tip (#804) with the calamansi cream.

3. Pipe a small amount of the cream into the bottom portion of the chou [13]; remove the frozen blackberry cream dome from the silicone mold; place it in the center of the cream [14]. Pipe more calamansi cream on top [15].

Note: You can pipe the blackberry cream directly into the chou if the blackberry cream is not frozen in dome-shaped silicone molds.

4. Fill another large pastry bag (45.7-cm/18-in) fitted with a 1-cm/0.38-in plain tip (#804) with the Italian meringue.

5. Pipe the meringue on top of the calamansi cream in circular spirals to form a cone shape [16]. Lightly brown the meringue on all sides using a propane torch [17].

PEANUT BUTTER AND CARAMELIZED BANANA

The familiar pair of peanut butter and banana is transformed into a sophisticated pastry with peanut-crumble topped choux, creamy peanut butter mousseline cream, and rum-flavored caramelized bananas. This rich and decadent dessert may have a similar flavor profile as an ordinary peanut butter-banana sandwich, but it will be the most delicious "peanut butter-banana sandwich" you have ever tasted!

Yield: about 12 choux pastries

INGREDIENTS

Triple Choux with Peanut-Crumble Topping:

50 g/1.8 oz all-purpose flour

50 g/1.8 oz finely ground peanuts

50 g/1.8 oz light brown sugar

Pinch of kosher salt or fine sea salt

50 g/1.8 oz unsalted butter cubes, at room temperature

1 recipe pâte à choux (page 12)

Caramelized Bananas:

60 g/2.1 oz unsalted butter

60 g/2.1 oz light brown sugar

400 g/14.1 oz peeled bananas, sliced

30 g/1.1 oz (2 Tbsp) dark rum

Peanut Butter Mousseline Cream:

400 g/14.1 oz pastry cream (page 17)

170 g/6 oz peanut butter

230 g/8.1 oz unsalted butter, at room temperature

Assembly and Decoration:

Powdered sugar

Triple Choux with Peanut-Crumble Topping:

1. Combine the flour, ground peanuts, light brown sugar, and salt in a food processor. Pulse the food processor a few times to evenly distribute the ingredients.

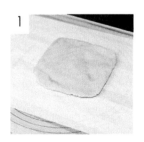

2. Add the soft butter pieces. Pulse the machine a few more times until a smooth dough forms. Do not over-mix.

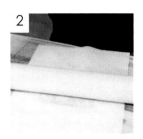

3 Place the dough between two pieces of plastic wrap and flatten the dough slightly. Chill for two hours in the refrigerator.

4. Roll out the dough between two pieces of parchment paper to 2-mm/0.08-in thick [1, 2]. Chill the dough in the refrigerator for about 45 minutes or in the freezer for about 10 minutes.

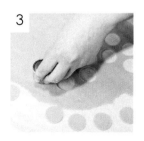

5. Remove the chilled dough from the refrigerator or freezer. Use a 2.8-cm/1.1-in round pastry cutter to cut out circular disks from the dough [3]. Return the cookie disks to the refrigerator or freezer until ready to use.

6. Preheat the oven to 191°C/375°F. Follow the directions on page 12 to make the choux paste.

7. Fill a large pastry bag (45.7-cm/18-in) fitted with a 1.7-cm/0.69-in plain tip (#809) with the choux paste. Pipe the paste into a 3.8-cm/1.5-in mound; pipe two more mounds right below the first mound along a straight line [4]. Make sure the three mounds are touching.

8. Brush the piped choux with egg wash using a gentle dabbing motion [5]. Place the peanut-crumble disks on top of the piped mounds [6].

9. Bake at 191°C/375°F for 18 to 20 minutes until the choux are puffed up. Reduce the temperature to 177°C/350°F and bake for another 15 minutes until the choux are golden brown. Turn off the oven and leave the choux in the oven undisturbed for another 10 minutes. Remove the baked choux from the oven and let cool completely.

Caramelized Bananas:

1. Melt the butter in a medium-sized stainless steel sauté pan. When the melted butter starts to sizzle, add the sugar and banana slices. Gently spread the banana slices in an even layer using a spatula [7].

2. Cook the mixture over medium heat until the banana slices are browned on one side. Turn the banana slices over and continue to cook until they are caramelized.

3. Pour in the dark rum to deglaze the pan [8]. Cook the mixture for another minute to allow the alcohol to evaporate. Let cool completely before using.

Peanut Butter Mousseline Cream:

1. Combine the pastry cream (page 17) with peanut butter in a mixer bowl. Beat with a stand mixer fitted with a wire whisk attachment on medium-high speed until the mixture is smooth.

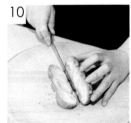

2. Reduce the mixer speed to medium-low and whisk in the soft butter in small increments. Make sure each addition of butter is thoroughly incorporated before adding more butter. Scrape down the sides of the bowl with a spatula if necessary. Once all the butter is incorporated, adjust the mixer to medium-high speed. Continue to beat for a few more minutes until the cream is light and fluffy [9].

Assembly and Decoration:

1. Using a serrated knife, cut off the top ⅓ of each triple-choux [10] and reserve the cap.

2. Fill a large pastry bag (45.7-cm/18-in) fitted with a 1-cm/0.38-in fine star tip (#864) with the peanut butter mousseline cream.

3. Fill the bottom of the choux with caramelized bananas [11]. Pipe the peanut butter mousseline cream on top of the bananas [12]. Place the reserved cap of the triple-choux on top of the cream [13]. Dust the middle portion with powdered sugar if desired [14].

PINEAPPLE AND GUAVA

Escape to a tropical paradise with this exquisite tart composed of a crunchy almond tart shell, fresh pineapples, refreshing lime and white chocolate cream, topped with delightful guava cream-filled choux.

Yield: about 6 8-cm/3.1-in round tarts

INGREDIENTS

Lime and White Chocolate Cream:

500 g/17.6 oz heavy whipping cream

7 g/0.25 oz fresh lime zest from about 3 medium-sized limes

170 g/6 oz white chocolate couverture, finely chopped

40 g/1.4 oz fresh lime juice

Tart Shells:

6 8-cm/3.1-in round tart shells (page 22)

Guava Cream:

50 g/1.8 oz egg yolks

40 g/1.4 oz granulated sugar

20 g/0.71 oz cornstarch

230 g/8.1 oz pink guava puree

20 g/0.71 oz unsalted butter, at room temperature

40 g/1.4 oz heavy whipping cream

Mini Choux:

½ recipe (270 g/9.5 oz) pâte à choux (page 12)

Assembly and Decoration:

300 g/10.6 oz pastry fondant (page 21)

Lime and White Chocolate Cream:

1. Combine the cream and lime zest in a medium-sized stainless steel saucepan [1]. Bring the mixture to a boil. Remove from heat. Cover the pan and allow the mixture to infuse for about 10 minutes.

2. Meanwhile, place the white chocolate pieces in a mixing bowl. Gently melt the chocolate using a double-boiler. Stir occasionally to allow even heating. Remove the chocolate from the double-boiler when about 75% of the chocolate is melted [2]. Reserve.

3. Bring the infused cream back to a boil and strain over the melted chocolate using a fine mesh strainer [3]. Wait 30 seconds, and then stir the mixture until it is velvety smooth. Stir in the fresh lime juice.

4. Cover the surface of the soft ganache cream with plastic wrap. Allow the ganache cream to set in the refrigerator overnight.

Tart Shells:

Follow the directions on page 22 to make 6 8-cm/3.1-in round tart shells. Store the tart shells in an airtight container until ready to use.

Guava Cream:

1. Combine egg yolks, sugar, and cornstarch in a mixing bowl. Mix well with a whisk. Set aside.

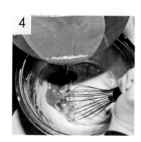

2. Heat the guava puree in a medium-sized stainless steel saucepan over medium-high heat. Remove from heat when the puree comes to a boil. Pour about half the puree into the reserved egg mixture while whisking vigorously [4]. Pour the

80 g/2.8 oz 30° Baume syrup (page 21)

Red gel food coloring

Fresh pineapple cubes

Crunchy white chocolate pearls

entire mixture back into the pan. Cook the mixture over medium-low heat while whisking constantly for 1 to 2 minutes until the mixture thickens. Cover the surface of the guava mixture with plastic wrap and let cool completely.

3. Whisk the guava mixture with softened butter in a stand mixer until the mixture is smooth and light.

4. Whisk the chilled heavy cream to medium-soft peaks; gently fold the whipped cream into the guava mixture [5]. Reserve the filling in the refrigerator until ready to use.

Mini Choux:

Follow the directions on page 12 to make about 25 to 30 3.8-cm/1.5-in mini choux. When the baked choux are completely cooled, use a 0.8-cm/0.31-in fine star tip (#863) to punch a hole in the bottom of each chou.

Assembly and Decoration:

1. Fill a large pastry bag (45.7-cm/18-in) fitted with a 0.6-cm/0.25-in plain tip (#802) with the guava cream. Pipe a small amount of the guava cream into each chou through the hole in the bottom [6]. Repeat until all the choux are filled.

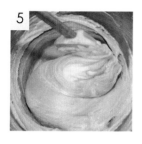
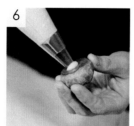

2. In a medium-sized mixing bowl, combine the pastry fondant, 30° Baume syrup, and a drop of red food coloring. Gently heat the mixture over a double-boiler or in a microwave until the mixture reaches 37°C/99°F. Do not heat the mixture hotter than 50°C/122°F.

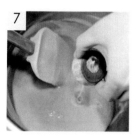

3. Dip the filled chou into the diluted pastry fondant [7]. Gently shake off excess glaze and place the chou bottom-side down on a piece of parchment paper. Repeat until all the choux are glazed.

4. Whisk the lime and white chocolate cream in a stand mixer fitted with a whisk attachment until stiff peaks form.

5. Fill the bottom of the prepared tart shell with a thin layer of lime and white chocolate cream [8]. Add fresh pineapple cubes [9] and then add more lime and white chocolate cream on top. Use a small offset spatula to level the cream [10]. Place three guava cream-filled mini choux on top of the filled tart shell.

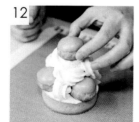

6. Fill a large pastry bag (45.7-cm/18-in) fitted with a 1.3-cm/0.5-in closed star tip (#846) with the remaining lime and white chocolate cream. Pipe the lime and white chocolate cream between adjacent choux [11] and on top of the choux. Place another mini chou on top [12]. Decorate the chou with a crunchy white chocolate pearl if desired.

BLUEBERRY, MEYER LEMON, AND OATS

This pastry is inspired by my favorite everyday breakfast—warm oatmeal with homemade Meyer lemon marmalade and fresh blueberries. The addition of oats in the choux paste brings a rustic and earthy dimension to the pastry; together with the blueberry and Meyer lemon cream, this ordinary breakfast combination has been transformed into an extraordinary chou creation!

Yield: about 14 14-cm/5.5-in éclairs

INGREDIENTS

Blueberry and Meyer Lemon Cream:

4 g/0.14 oz gelatin sheet (silver grade) or 3.4 g/0.12 oz powdered gelatin + 20.4 g/0.72 oz cold water

150 g/5.3 oz blueberry puree

15 g/0.53 oz (1 Tbsp) fresh Meyer lemon juice

45 g/1.6 oz granulated sugar

150 g/5.3 oz cream cheese, at room temperature

150 g/5.3 oz heavy whipping cream

Oatmeal Éclairs:

30 g/1.1 oz old-fashion rolled oats

90 g/3.2 oz bread flour

100 g/3.5 oz distilled water

100 g/3.5 oz whole milk

2 g/0.071 oz (¼ tsp) kosher salt or fine sea salt

5 g /0.18 oz (1 tsp) granulated sugar

80 g/2.8 oz unsalted butter

Blueberry and Meyer Lemon Cream:

1. In a medium-sized bowl, bloom the sheet gelatin in plenty of cold water. If powdered gelatin is used, sprinkle the powder over 20.4 g/0.72 oz cold water in the bowl. Let the gelatin bloom for at least 10 minutes before using.

2. Combine the blueberry puree, Meyer lemon juice, and sugar in a medium-sized stainless steel saucepan. Mix well with a balloon whisk. Bring the mixture to 71°C/160°F over medium-high heat. Let cool slightly.

3. Meanwhile, squeeze excess water out of the bloomed sheet gelatin and add the gelatin to the blueberry mixture [1]. If powdered gelatin is used, add the entire contents to the blueberry mixture. Stir to combine. Cover the surface of the blueberry jelly with plastic wrap. Let cool completely.

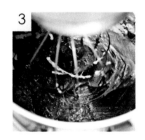

4. In a stand mixer fitted with a whisk attachment, whisk the softened cream cheese until smooth [2]. Gradually add the blueberry jelly and whisk until the mixture is smooth and homogenous [3]. Chill the blueberry-cream cheese mixture in the refrigerator for 30 minutes to an hour.

5. In a stand mixer fitted with a whisk attachment, whisk the chilled heavy cream to medium peaks. Gently fold the whipped cream into the blueberry-cream cheese mixture until well combined [4]. Reserve the cream in the refrigerator until ready to use.

200 g/7.1 oz whole eggs

1 whole egg for egg wash

Assembly and Decoration:

300 g/10.6 oz pastry fondant (page 21)

15 g/0.53 oz (1 Tbsp) fresh Meyer lemon juice

60 g/2.1 oz 30° Baume syrup (page 21)

Yellow gel food coloring (optional)

Fresh blueberries

Blueberry nuggets or dried blueberries

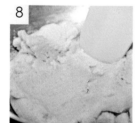

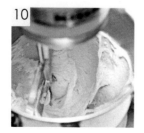

Oatmeal Éclairs:

1. Place the rolled oats in a coffee grinder and grind the oats into a fine powder [5, 6].

2. Sift the bread flour and ground oats onto a piece of parchment paper. Transfer the sifted flour and oats to a bowl and reserve.

3. Combine the water, milk, salt, sugar, and butter in a large stainless steel saucepan; heat the mixture over medium-high heat.

4. When the mixture comes to a boil, remove the saucepan from heat. Carefully whisk the sifted flour mixture into the hot liquid [7]. When all the flour mixture is incorporated into the liquid, shake off lumps of dough from the whisk and switch to a spatula or wooden spoon.

5. Return the saucepan to medium-low heat. Continue to cook for 2 to 3 minutes; stir constantly, using a folding motion to eliminate any remaining small lumps of flour and bring the dough pieces together. Cook until a smooth and thick paste is obtained [8].

6. Transfer the dough to a mixer bowl. Attach the bowl to a mixer that is fitted with a paddle attachment. Mix the dough at medium speed for 10 to 15 seconds to release the steam.

7. Add the eggs one at a time while continuing to mix on medium speed [9]. Make sure each egg is incorporated before adding additional eggs. Scrape down the sides of the mixer bowl with a spatula if necessary. Increase the mixer speed to high. Mix for 10 to 20 seconds or until a smooth paste forms [10].

8. Meanwhile, line a half-sheet baking pan with a silicone baking mat or parchment paper. Preheat the oven to 191°C/375°F. Fill a large pastry bag (45.7-cm/18-in) fitted with a 1.3-cm/0.5-in fine star tip (#866) with the choux paste. Pipe the paste into 14-cm/5.5-in logs with 2.5-cm/1-in spacing on the baking mat or parchment paper [11]. Brush the top with egg wash using a gentle dabbing motion [12].

9. Bake at 191°C/375°F for about 18 minutes until the éclairs are puffed up. Reduce the temperature to 177°C/350°F and bake for another 15 minutes until the éclairs are golden brown. Turn off the oven and leave the éclairs in the oven undisturbed for another 10 minutes. Remove the baked éclairs from the oven [13].

10. When the baked éclairs are completely cooled, use a 1-cm/0.38-in fine star tip (#864) to punch three holes in the bottom of each éclair [14].

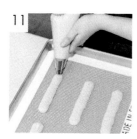

Assembly and Decoration:

1. Fill a large pastry bag (45.7-cm/18-in) fitted with a 0.8-cm/0.31-in plain tip (#803) with the blueberry and Meyer lemon cream. Pipe the cream into each éclair through the holes in the bottom [15, 16].

2. To make the lemon fondant glaze, in a medium-sized mixing bowl, combine the pastry fondant, Meyer lemon juice, and 30° Baume syrup. Add a small amount of yellow gel coloring into the mixture if desired. Gently heat the mixture over a double-boiler or in a microwave until the mixture reaches 37°C/99°F. Do not heat the mixture hotter than 50°C/122°F.

3. Dip the filled éclair into the lemon fondant glaze [17, 18]. Gently shake off excess glaze and place the éclair bottom-side down on a piece of parchment paper. Repeat until all the éclairs are glazed.

4. Decorate the éclairs with fresh blueberries and blueberry nuggets if desired [19, 20].

WALNUT AND CHOCOLATE

This delightful tart is composed of caramelized walnuts, chocolate pastry cream, and walnut choux. The walnut oil-based choux paste gives this pastry an unusual nutty twist. Although the walnut-crumble topping on its own is the ideal addition to the walnut choux, a combination of different glazes can offer an interesting variety to this elegant tart.

Yield: 5 10-cm/3.9-in round tarts

INGREDIENTS

Tart Shells:

5 10-cm/3.9-in round tart shells (page 22)

Walnut-Crumble Topping:

50 g/1.8 oz all-purpose flour

50 g/1.8 oz finely ground walnuts

50 g/1.8 oz light brown sugar

Pinch of kosher salt or fine sea salt

50 g/1.8 oz unsalted butter cubes, at room temperature

Walnut Mini Choux:

120 g/4.2 oz all-purpose flour

180 g/6.3 oz distilled water

80 g/2.8 oz walnut oil

2 g/0.071 oz (¼ tsp) kosher salt or fine sea salt

5 g /0.18 oz (1 tsp) granulated sugar

200 g/7.1 oz whole eggs

1 whole egg for egg wash

Caramelized Walnuts:

200 g/7.1 oz granulated sugar

Tart Shells:

Follow the directions on page 22 to make 5 10-cm/3.9-in round tart shells. Store the tart shells in an airtight container until ready to use.

Walnut-Crumble Topping:

1. Combine the flour, ground walnuts, light brown sugar, and salt in a food processor. Pulse the food processor a few times to evenly distribute the ingredients.

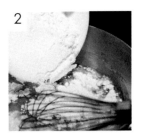

2. Add the soft butter pieces. Pulse the machine a few more times until a smooth dough forms. Do not over-mix.

3. Place the dough between two pieces of plastic wrap and flatten the dough slightly. Chill for 2 hours in the refrigerator.

4. Roll out the dough between two pieces of parchment paper to 2-mm/0.08-in thick. Chill the dough in the refrigerator for about 45 minutes or in the freezer for about 10 minutes.

5. Remove the chilled dough from the refrigerator or freezer. Use a 2.2-cm/0.9-in round pastry cutter to cut out circular disks from the dough. Return the cookie disks to the refrigerator or freezer until ready to use.

Walnut Mini Choux:

1. For the walnut choux paste, sift the flour onto a piece of parchment paper. Transfer the sifted flour to a bowl and reserve.

110 g/3.9 oz distilled water

250 g/8.8 oz walnut pieces

Chocolate Mousseline Cream:

530 g/18.7 oz chocolate pastry cream (page 18)

100 g/3.5 oz unsalted butter, at room temperature

Assembly and Decoration:

Walnut halves (optional)

Dipping caramel (page 19) (optional)

Chocolate glaze (page 20) (optional)

Pastry fondant (page 21) (optional)

2. Combine the water, walnut oil, salt, and sugar in a large stainless steel saucepan; heat the mixture over medium-high heat.

3. When the mixture comes to a boil [1], remove the saucepan from heat. Carefully whisk the sifted flour into the mixture [2]. When all the flour is incorporated into the liquid, shake off lumps of dough from the whisk and switch to a spatula or wooden spoon.

4. Return the saucepan to medium-low heat. Continue to cook for 2 to 3 minutes; stir constantly, using a folding motion to eliminate any remaining small lumps of flour and bring the dough pieces together. Cook until a smooth and thick paste is obtained.

5. Transfer the dough to a mixer bowl. Attach the bowl to a mixer fitted with a paddle attachment. Mix the dough at medium speed for 10 to 15 seconds to release the steam.

6. Add the eggs one at a time while continuing to mix on medium speed. Make sure each egg is incorporated before adding additional eggs. Scrape down the sides of the mixer bowl with a spatula if necessary. Increase the mixer speed to high. Mix for 10 to 20 seconds or until a smooth paste forms.

7. Meanwhile, line a half-sheet baking pan with a silicone baking mat or parchment paper. Preheat the oven to 191°C/375°F. Fill a large pastry bag (45.7-cm/18-in) fitted with a 1.3-cm/0.5-in plain tip (#806) with the choux paste. Pipe the paste into 2.5-cm/1-in mounds with 2.5-cm/1-in spacing on the baking mat or parchment paper. Brush the top with egg wash using a gentle dabbing motion [3]. Place the walnut crumble cookie disks on top of the piped choux paste [4].

8. Bake at 191°C/375°F for about 13 minutes until the choux are puffed up. Reduce the temperature to 177°C/350°F and bake for another 13 minutes until the choux are golden brown. Turn off the oven and leave the choux in the oven undisturbed for another 8 minutes. Remove the baked choux from the oven [5].

9. When the baked choux are completely cooled, use a 0.8-cm/0.31-in fine star tip (#863) to punch a hole in the bottom of each chou.

Caramelized Walnuts:

1. In a medium-sized stainless stain saucepan, combine the sugar and water. Bring the mixture to a boil over medium-high heat.

2. Add the walnut pieces [6] and reduce the heat to medium. Stir constantly; cook for about 8 to 10 minutes until the liquid evaporates and the sugar becomes crystallized [7].

3. Reduce the heat to low; continue to stir for another 2 to 3 minutes until the white sugar crystals turn to dark brown caramel [8].

4. Spread the caramelized walnuts on a silicone mat or parchment paper. Cool completely before using.

Chocolate Mousseline Cream:

1. Place the chocolate pastry cream (page 18) in a mixer bowl. Beat with a stand mixer fitted with a wire whisk attachment on medium-high speed until the mixture is smooth.

2. Reduce the mixer speed to medium-low and whisk in the soft butter in small increments. Make sure each addition of butter is thoroughly incorporated before adding more butter. Scrape down the sides of the bowl with a spatula if necessary.

3. Once all the butter is incorporated, adjust the mixer to medium-high speed. Continue to beat for a few more minutes until the cream is light and fluffy [9].

Assembly and Decoration:

1. *Optional*: To make the candied walnut decoration, insert toothpicks (with two sharp ends) into the walnut halves and set aside [10, 11]. Prepare the dipping caramel (page 19). Hold the toothpick and carefully dip the walnut half into the hot caramel [12]. Insert the holding end of the toothpick into a tall Styrofoam piece [13]. Allow the caramel to harden until ready to use [14].

2. Meanwhile, fill a large pastry bag (45.7-cm/18-in) fitted with a 0.6-cm/0.25-in plain tip (#802) with the chocolate pastry cream. Pipe a small amount of cream into each walnut chou through the hole in the bottom. If desired, coat the filled choux with dipping caramel (page 19), chocolate glaze (page 20), or pastry fondant (page 21).

3. Fill the bottom of the prepared tart shell with a thin layer of chocolate mousseline cream [15]. Sprinkle caramelized walnuts [16] and then add more chocolate cream on top. Use a small offset spatula to level the cream [17]. Place five filled walnut choux on top of the filled tart shell along the outer edge [18].

4. Fill another large pastry bag (45.7-cm/18-in) fitted with a 1.3-cm/0.5-in closed star tip (#846) with the remaining chocolate mousseline cream.

5. Pipe more chocolate cream between adjacent choux and on top of the choux [19]. Decorate the top with a candied walnut half if desired [20].

APRICOT AND ALMOND MASCARPONE

This pastry features an ensemble of almond components. The triple-almond choux contain almond flour in both the crumble-cookie topping and choux paste. The use of almond oil in the choux paste provides the pastry with an extra crunchiness and a lighter texture. In the double-almond cream, almond paste is paired with amaretto liqueur to emphasize the almond flavor. Without a doubt, this is the ultimate pastry for any almond lover.

Yield: 12 7.6-cm/3-in individual pastries

INGREDIENTS

Apricot Cream:

2.5 g/0.088 oz gelatin sheet (silver grade) or 2.1 g/0.074 oz powdered gelatin + 12.6 g/0.44 oz cold water

230 g/8.1 oz apricot puree

40 g/1.4 oz granulated sugar

15 g/0.53 oz cornstarch

Triple-Almond Choux:

200 g/7.1 oz crumble-cookie topping (page 16)

100 g/3.5 oz bread flour

20 g/0.71 oz almond flour

180 g/6.3 oz distilled water

70 g/2.5 oz sweet almond oil

2 g/0.071 oz (¼ tsp) kosher salt or fine sea salt

5 g /0.18 oz (1 tsp) granulated sugar

180 g/6.3 oz whole eggs

1 whole egg for egg wash

Apricot Cream:

1. In a medium-sized bowl, bloom the sheet gelatin in plenty of cold water. If powdered gelatin is used, sprinkle the powder over 12.6 g/0.44 oz cold water in the bowl. Let the gelatin bloom for at least 10 minutes before using.

2. Combine the apricot puree, sugar, and cornstarch in a medium-sized stainless steel saucepan. Mix well with a balloon whisk [1]. Bring the mixture to a boil over medium-high heat while whisking constantly. Remove from heat when the mixture thickens. Let cool slightly.

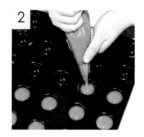

3. Meanwhile, squeeze excess water out of the bloomed sheet gelatin and add the gelatin to the apricot mixture. If powdered gelatin is used, add the entire contents to the apricot mixture. Stir to combine. Cover the surface of the apricot cream with plastic wrap. Let cool completely.

4. Fill a large pastry bag (45.7-cm/18-in) fitted with a 1-cm/0.38-in plain tip (#804) with the apricot cream. Pipe the cream into the cavities of 3-cm/1.2-in half-sphere silicone molds [2]. Place the filled molds in the freezer until ready to use.

Note: The silicone molds keep the apricot cream filling in perfect dome shape, which makes an impressive presentation in the finished desserts. You can omit this step if silicone molds are not available.

Triple-Almond Choux:

1. Follow the directions on page 16 to make the crumble-cookie topping. Roll out the dough be-

Double-Almond Cream:

50 g/1.8 oz heavy whipping cream (A)

100 g/3.5 oz almond paste

20 g/0.71 oz amaretto liqueur

450 g/15.9 oz heavy whipping cream (B)

50 g/1.8 oz granulated sugar

250 g/8.8 oz mascarpone cheese

Assembly and Decoration:

Apricot nuggets or diced dried apricots

Powdered sugar

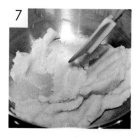

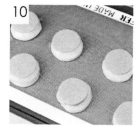

tween two pieces of parchment paper to 2-mm/0.08-in thick [3]. Chill the dough in the refrigerator for about 45 minutes or in the freezer for about 10 minutes.

2. Remove the chilled dough from the refrigerator or freezer. Use a 5-cm/2-in round pastry cutter to cut out circular disks from the dough [4]. Return the cookie disks to the refrigerator or freezer until ready to use.

3. For the almond choux paste, sift the bread flour and almond flour onto a piece of parchment paper [5]. Transfer the sifted flours to a bowl and reserve.

4. Combine the water, almond oil, salt, and sugar in a large stainless steel saucepan; heat the mixture over medium-high heat.

5. When the mixture comes to a boil, remove the saucepan from heat. Carefully whisk the sifted flour mixture into the hot liquid [6]. When all the flour mixture is incorporated into the liquid, shake off lumps of dough from the whisk and switch to a spatula or wooden spoon.

6. Return the saucepan to medium-low heat. Continue to cook for 2 to 3 minutes; stir constantly, using a folding motion to eliminate any remaining small lumps of flour and bring the dough pieces together. Cook until a smooth and thick paste is obtained [7].

7. Transfer the dough to a mixer bowl. Attach the bowl to a mixer fitted with a paddle attachment. Mix the dough at medium speed for 10 to 15 seconds to release the steam.

8. Add the eggs one at a time while continuing to mix on medium speed [8]. Make sure each egg is incorporated before adding additional eggs. Scrape down the sides of the mixer bowl with a spatula if necessary. Increase the mixer speed to high. Mix for 10 to 20 seconds or until a smooth paste forms.

9. Meanwhile, line a half-sheet baking pan with a silicone baking mat or parchment paper. Preheat the oven to 191°C/375°F. Fill a large pastry bag (45.7-cm/18-in) fitted with a 1.7-cm/0.69-in plain tip (#809) with the choux paste. Pipe the paste into 6.4-cm/2.5-in mounds with 2.5-cm/1-in spacing on the baking mat or parchment paper [9]. Brush the top with egg wash using a gentle dabbing motion. Place the crumble-cookie disks on top of the piped choux paste [10].

10. Bake at 191°C/375°F for about 20 minutes until the choux are puffed up. Reduce the temperature to 177°C/350°F and bake for another 20 minutes until the choux are golden brown. Turn off the oven and leave the choux in the oven undisturbed for another 10 minutes. Remove the baked choux from the oven and let cool completely [11].

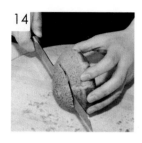

Double-Almond Cream:

1. Combine heavy cream (A), almond paste, and amaretto liqueur in a small stainless steel saucepan. Heat the mixture over medium-low heat.

2. Use a spatula to smooth the almond paste mixture until it is homogenous [12]. Remove from heat. Cover the surface of the mixture with plastic wrap and let cool completely.

3. Place the smoothed almond paste mixture, heavy cream (B), sugar, and the mascarpone cheese in a mixer bowl. Attach the bowl to a stand mixer fitted with a whisk attachment.

4. Whisk the mixture on medium speed until it thickens. Increase the speed to high and continue to whisk until stiff peaks form [13]. Place the almond cream in the refrigerator until ready to use.

Assembly and Decoration:

1. Using a serrated knife, cut off the top ⅓ of each chou [14] and reserve the cap.

2. Fill a large pastry bag (45.7-cm/18-in) fitted with a 1.4-cm/0.56-in closed star tip (#847) with the almond cream.

3. Pipe a small amount of the cream into the bottom portion of the chou [15]; remove the frozen apricot cream dome from the silicone mold and place it in the center of the cream [16]. Pipe more almond cream on top [17].

Note: You can pipe the apricot cream directly into the chou if the apricot cream is not frozen in dome-shaped silicone molds.

4. Decorate with apricot nuggets or diced dried apricots [18]. Place the reserved cap on top of the cream. Dust the top with powdered sugar if desired [19].

PISTACHIO AND STRAWBERRY

This is my mother's favorite pastry. The strawberry cream-filled choux coated with sweet and crunchy caramel remind her of her childhood in Beijing. When she was a little girl growing up in Beijing, her favorite snack was the caramel covered fruits sold by small vendors at markets. Of course, her beloved childhood snack has been elevated into a refined pastry—crunchy tart shell filled with rich and velvety pistachio mousseline cream, strawberry cream-filled choux, and fresh strawberries.

Yield: 5 10-cm/3.9-in round tarts

INGREDIENTS

Tart Shells:

5 10-cm/3.9-in round tart shells (page 22)

Strawberry Cream:

50 g/1.8 oz egg yolks

40 g/1.4 oz granulated sugar

20 g/0.71 oz cornstarch

230 g/8.1 oz strawberry puree

20 g/0.71 oz unsalted butter, at room temperature

40 g/1.4 oz heavy whipping cream

Mini Choux:

½ recipe (270 g/9.5 oz) pâte à choux (page 12)

Pistachio Mousseline Cream:

330 g/11.6 oz pastry cream (page 17)

120 g/4.2 oz pistachio paste

Green gel food coloring

200 g/7.1 oz unsalted butter, at room temperature

Tart Shells:

Follow the directions on page 22 to make 5 10-cm/3.9-in round tart shells. Store the tart shells in an airtight container until ready to use.

Strawberry Cream:

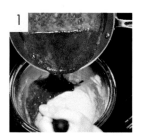

1. Combine egg yolks, sugar, and cornstarch in a mixing bowl. Mix well with a whisk. Set aside.

2. Heat the strawberry puree in a medium-sized stainless steel saucepan over medium-high heat. Remove from heat when the puree comes to a boil. Pour about half the puree into the reserved egg mixture while whisking vigorously [1]. Pour the entire mixture back into the pan.

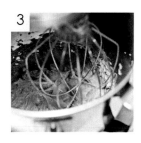

3. Cook the mixture over medium-low heat while whisking constantly for 1 to 2 minutes until the mixture thickens [2]. Cover the surface of the strawberry mixture with plastic wrap and let cool completely.

4. Whisk the strawberry mixture with softened butter in a stand mixer until the mixture is smooth and light [3].

5. Whisk the chilled heavy cream to medium-soft peaks; gently fold the whipped cream into the strawberry mixture [4]. Reserve the filling in the refrigerator until ready to use.

Assembly and Decoration:

Dipping caramel (page 19)

Red gel food coloring

Fresh strawberries, chopped and in wedges

Chopped pistachios

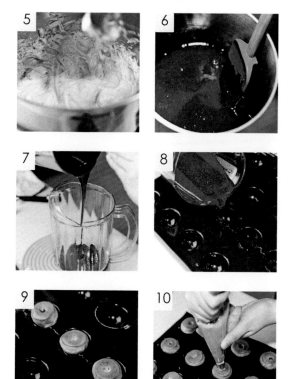

Mini Choux:

Follow the directions on page 12 to make about 25 to 30 3.8-cm/1.5-in mini choux. When the baked choux are completely cooled, use a 0.8-cm/0.31-in fine star tip (#863) to punch a hole in the bottom of each chou.

Pistachio Mousseline Cream:

1. Combine the pastry cream (page 17) with the pistachio paste in a mixer bowl. Add a few drops of green food coloring if desired. Beat with a stand mixer fitted with a wire whisk attachment on medium-high speed until the mixture is smooth.

2. Reduce the mixer speed to medium-low and whisk in the soft butter in small increments. Make sure each addition of butter is thoroughly incorporated before adding more. Scrape down the sides of the bowl with a spatula if necessary.

3. Once all the butter is incorporated, adjust the mixer to medium-high speed. Continue to beat for a few more minutes until the cream is light and fluffy [5].

Assembly and Decoration:

1. Follow the directions on page 19 to make the dipping caramel. When the caramel reaches the desired temperature, remove from heat. Add a few drops of red food coloring and stir to combine [6]. Allow the bubbles to subside slightly. Transfer the caramel to a heat-proof pitcher [7] and then pour a small amount of caramel into the cavities of 4.1-cm/1.6-in half-sphere silicone molds to about ⅓ full [8].

2. Quickly insert the choux into caramel-filled molds with the bottom-side up [9]. Let the caramel harden completely before continuing.

Note: If silicone molds are not available, you can dip the choux directly into the caramel and place the glazed choux on a silicone baking mat or a piece of parchment paper with the caramel-coated side down.

3. Fill a large pastry bag (45.7-cm/18-in) fitted with a 0.6-cm/0.25-in plain tip (#802) with the strawberry cream. Pipe a small amount of strawberry cream into each chou through the hole in the bottom [10]. Carefully remove the filled choux from the silicone molds.

4. Fill the bottom of the prepared tart shell with a thin layer of pistachio mousseline cream [11]. Add fresh strawberry pieces [12] and then add more pistachio cream on top. Use a small offset spatula to level the cream [13]. Place five strawberry cream-filled mini choux on top of the filled tart shell along the outer edge [14].

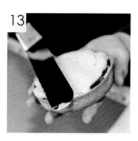

5. Fill another large pastry bag (45.7-cm/18-in) fitted with a medium-sized St. Honoré tip (3-cm/1.2-in opening) with the remaining pistachio cream.

6. Pipe the pistachio mousseline cream between adjacent choux [15]. Arrange fresh strawberry wedges in the center and sprinkle the top with chopped pistachios [16].

FUNNY

BUNNY (CARROT CREAM-CHEESE)

This whimsical pastry brings a smile to everyone's face. Sweet and tangy carrot cream-filled choux, with just a hint of spices, are presented on a crispy and buttery puff pastry base. The marzipan bunny ears and carrots add a playful touch to this lovely dessert.

Yield: about 30 individual pastries

INGREDIENTS

Puff Pastry Base:

600 g/21.2 oz puff pastry dough (page 24)

Granulated sugar for dusting

Powdered sugar for dusting

Mini Choux:

100 g/3.5 oz crumble-cookie topping (page 16)

½ recipe (270 g/9.5 oz) pâte à choux (page 12)

Carrot Cream-Cheese Filling:

5 g/0.18 oz gelatin sheet (silver grade) or 4.2 g/0.15 oz powdered gelatin + 25.2 g/0.89 oz cold water

150 g/5.3 oz carrot juice

0.25 g/0.0088 oz (⅛ tsp) cardamom powder

0.25 g/0.0088 oz (⅛ tsp) cinnamon powder

50 g/1.8 oz granulated sugar

150 g/5.3 oz cream cheese, at room temperature

180 g/6.3 oz heavy whipping cream

Assembly and Decoration:

300 g/10.6 oz pastry fondant (page 21)

Puff Pastry Base:

1. Roll out the puff pastry dough (page 24) to about 3-mm/0.1-in thick. Allow the dough to rest in the refrigerator for 15 minutes. Dock the dough with a dough docker or fork. Cut the dough into 10-cm x 3.8-cm/4-in x 1.5-in rectangles.

2. Place the puff pastry rectangles on a half-sheet baking pan lined with a silicone baking mat or parchment paper [1]. Loosely cover the pan with plastic wrap and allow the dough to rest in the refrigerator for an hour.

3. Preheat the oven to 191°C/375°F. Sprinkle the puff pastry dough with granulated sugar [2]. To prevent the puff pastries from puffing up too much, place another piece of parchment paper or silicone mat on the dough and then place a cooling rack on top [3, 4].

4. Bake for about 25 minutes until the pastries are light golden brown. Remove the cooling rack and silicone mat or parchment paper [5]. Dust the puff pastries with powdered sugar [6].

5. Bake at 218°C/425°F for 3 to 5 minutes until the pastries are caramelized on top. Let cool completely before using [7].

Mini Choux:

1. Follow the directions on page 16 to make the crumble-cookie topping.

2. Roll out the dough between two pieces of parchment paper to 2-mm/0.08-in thick. Chill the dough in the refrigerator for about 45 minutes or in the freezer for about 10 minutes.

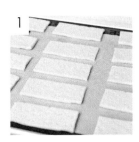

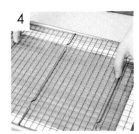

80 g/2.8 oz 30° Baume syrup (page 21)

Marzipan

Orange gel food coloring

Green gel food coloring

Red gel food coloring

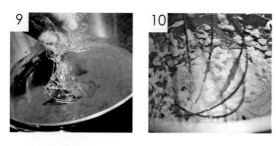

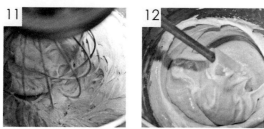

3. Remove the chilled dough from the refrigerator or freezer. Use a 2.2-cm/0.9-in round pastry cutter to cut out circular disks from the dough. Return the cookie disks back to the refrigerator or freezer until ready to use.

4. Follow the directions on page 12 to make round mini choux. Just before baking, place the crumble-cookie disks on top of the piped choux paste. Bake the choux according to the directions on page 13.

5. When the baked choux are completely cooled, use a 0.8-cm/0.31-in fine star tip (#863) to punch a hole in the bottom of each chou.

Carrot Cream-Cheese Filling:

1. In a medium-sized bowl, bloom the sheet gelatin in plenty of cold water. If powdered gelatin is used, sprinkle the powder over 25.2 g/0.89 oz cold water in the bowl. Let the gelatin bloom for at least 10 minutes before using.

2. Combine the carrot juice, cardamom and cinnamon powders, and sugar in a medium-sized stainless steel saucepan [8]. Mix well with a balloon whisk. Bring the mixture to 71°C/160°F over medium-high heat. Let cool slightly.

3. Meanwhile, squeeze excess water out of the bloomed sheet gelatin and add the gelatin to the carrot mixture [9]. If powdered gelatin is used, add the entire contents to the carrot mixture. Stir to combine. Cover the surface of the carrot jelly with plastic wrap. Let cool completely.

4. In a stand mixer fitted with a whisk attachment, whisk the softened cream cheese until smooth [10]. Gradually add the carrot jelly and whisk until the mixture is smooth and homogenous [11]. Chill the carrot-cream cheese mixture in the refrigerator for 30 minutes to an hour.

5. In a stand mixer fitted with a whisk attachment, whisk the chilled heavy cream to medium peaks. Gently fold the whipped cream into the carrot-cream cheese mixture until well combined [12]. Reserve the cream in the refrigerator until ready to use.

Assembly and Decoration:

1. Fill a large pastry bag (45.7-cm/18-in) fitted with a 0.6-cm/0.25-in plain tip (#802) with the carrot-cream cheese filling. Pipe the cream into each chou through the hole in the bottom.

2. To make the fondant glaze, in a medium-sized mixing bowl, combine the pastry fondant and 30° Baume syrup. Gently heat the mixture over a double-boiler or in a microwave until the mixture reaches 37°C/99°F. Do not heat the mixture hotter than 50°C/122°F.

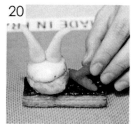

3. Dip the filled chou into the fondant glaze [13]. Gently shake off excess glaze and place the chou bottom-side down on a piece of parchment paper. Repeat until all the choux are glazed.

4. Take three large pieces of marzipan and color them orange, green, and pink. Cover with plastic wrap until ready to use.

5. Take two small pieces of natural-color marzipan and shape them into teardrops [14]. Flatten the pieces. Take two smaller pieces of pink marzipan and shape them into teardrops as well. Flatten the pink marzipan pieces and attach them to the natural-color marzipan pieces [15]. Bend them into rabbit ear shapes.

6. Take two pieces of orange marzipan and shape them into carrots [16]. Use a marzipan tool to make some fine lines [17]. Use two small pieces of green marzipan to make the leaves and attach them to the stem end of the carrots [18].

7. Place a filled chou on top of the puff pastry base and place the marzipan ears on top of the chou [19]. Place the marzipan carrots next to the chou [20].

SCHOLAR (JASMINE TEA)

I have always thought of tea as a thinker's drink, maybe because my great-grandfather loved drinking tea and he was a scholar who taught ancient Chinese philosophy at Beijing University. I have to say that tea is my favorite beverage as well, in particular jasmine tea. With its soothing fragrance, it has just the right amount of potency to clear one's mind but without overwhelming the senses. I wonder whether drinking tea helps one to become a thinker or a thinker always prefers to drink tea. Perhaps that is something to ponder while enjoying this inspiring dessert.

Yield: about 30 individual pastries

INGREDIENTS

Jasmine Tea and Milk Chocolate Cream:

220 g/7.8 oz heavy whipping cream

5 g/0.18 oz jasmine loose tea

10 g/0.35 oz granulated sugar

70 g/2.5 oz milk chocolate couverture, finely chopped

Puff Pastry Base:

300 g/10.6 oz puff pastry dough (page 24)

Granulated sugar for dusting

Powdered sugar for dusting

Mini Choux:

100 g/3.5 oz crumble-cookie topping (page 16)

½ recipe (270 g/9.5 oz) pâte à choux (page 12)

Assembly and Decoration:

Chocolate glaze (page 20)

Marzipan

Black gel food coloring

Orange gel food coloring

Jasmine Tea and Milk Chocolate Cream:

1. Combine the cream, jasmine tea, and sugar in a medium-sized stainless steel saucepan. Bring the mixture to a boil [1]. Remove from heat. Cover the pan and allow the mixture to infuse for about 15 minutes.

2. Meanwhile, place the milk chocolate in a mixing bowl. Gently melt the chocolate using a double-boiler. Stir occasionally to allow even heating. Remove the chocolate from the double-boiler when about 75% of the chocolate is melted. Reserve.

3. Bring the infused cream back to a boil and strain over the melted chocolate using a fine mesh strainer [2]. Wait 30 seconds and then stir the mixture until it is velvety smooth [3]. Cover the surface of the soft ganache cream with plastic wrap. Allow the ganache cream to set in the refrigerator overnight.

Puff Pastry Base:

1. Roll out the puff pastry dough (page 24) to about 3-mm/0.1-in thick. Allow the dough to rest in the refrigerator for 15 minutes. Dock the dough with a dough docker or fork. Cut the dough into 10-cm x 3.8-cm/4-in x 1.5-in rectangles.

2. Place the puff pastry rectangles on a half-sheet baking pan lined with a silicone baking mat or parchment paper. Loosely cover the pan with plastic wrap and allow the dough to rest in the refrigerator for an hour.

3. Preheat the oven to 191°C/375°F. Sprinkle the puff pastry dough with granulated sugar. To prevent the puff pastries from puffing up too much, place another piece of parchment paper or silicone mat on the dough and then place a cooling rack on top.

4. Bake for about 25 minutes until the pastries are light golden brown. Remove the rack and silicone mat or parchment paper. Dust the puff pastries with powdered sugar. Bake at 218°C/425°F for 3 to 5 minutes until the pastries are caramelized on top [4]. Let cool completely before using.

Mini Choux:

1. Follow the directions on page 16 to make the crumble-cookie topping. Roll out the dough between two pieces of parchment paper to 2-mm/0.08-in thick. Chill the dough in the refrigerator for about 45 minutes or in the freezer for about 10 minutes.

2. Remove the chilled dough from the refrigerator or freezer. Use a 2.2-cm/0.9-in round pastry cutter to cut out circular disks from the dough. Return the cookie disks to the refrigerator or freezer until ready to use.

3. Follow the directions on page 12 to make round mini choux. Just before baking, place the crumble-cookie disks on top of the piped choux paste. Bake the choux according to the directions on page 13.

4. When the baked choux are completely cooled, use a 0.8-cm/0.31-in fine star tip (#863) to punch a hole in the bottom of each chou.

Assembly and Decoration:

1. Transfer the chilled jasmine and chocolate cream to a mixer bowl. Attach the bowl to a stand mixer fitted with a whisk attachment. Whisk the soft ganache cream on high speed until stiff peaks form.

2. Fill a large pastry bag (45.7-cm/18-in) fitted with a 0.6-cm/0.25-in plain tip (#802) with the jasmine and chocolate cream. Pipe the cream into each chou through the hole in the bottom.

3. If desired, fill a small parchment paper cornet with chocolate glaze (page 20); pipe a pair of eye glasses on each chou [5].

4. Meanwhile, take two large pieces of marzipan and color them black and orange. Cover with plastic wrap until ready to use.

5. Take a piece of black marzipan and flatten it with the palm of your hand. Cut the marzipan into a square that is about 3.8-cm x 3.8-cm/1.5-in x 1.5-in in size [6]. Take a small piece of black marzipan and roll it into a ball. Flatten the ball into a disk and bend the disk into the rim for the cap [7].

6. Take a small piece of orange marzipan and roll it into a thin rope to represent the tassel. Attach the tassel to the top of the cap with a small black marzipan disk [8].

7. Cut the puff pastry base in two pieces and place a filled chou on top of one piece of puff pastry base. Place the finished marzipan cap on top of the chou [9].

WITCH (PUMPKIN MASCARPONE)

A perfect pairing of spiced pumpkin and mascarpone cream makes this a splendid autumn pastry. Why not add a humorous touch with a marzipan witch's hat and cape to make it a hit at the next Halloween gathering?

Yield: about 10 individual pastries

INGREDIENTS

Mini and Large Choux:

200 g/7.1 oz crumble-cookie topping (page 16)

1 recipe pâte à choux (page 12)

Pumpkin and Spice Mascarpone Cream:

4 g/0.14 oz gelatin sheet (silver grade) or 3.4 g/0.12 oz powdered gelatin + 20.4 g/0.72 oz cold water

170 g/6 oz pumpkin puree

45 g/1.6 oz granulated sugar

0.25 g/0.0088 oz (⅛ tsp) cinnamon powder

0.25 g/0.0088 oz (⅛ tsp) nutmeg powder

150 g/5.3 oz mascarpone cheese, at room temperature

150 g/5.3 oz heavy whipping cream

Assembly and Decoration:

300 g/10.6 oz pastry fondant (page 21)

80 g/2.8 oz 30° Baume syrup (page 21)

Orange gel food coloring

Marzipan

Black gel food coloring

Mini and Large Choux:

1. Follow the directions on page 16 to make the crumble-cookie topping. Roll out the dough between two pieces of parchment paper to 2-mm/0.08-in thick. Chill the dough in the refrigerator for about 45 minutes or in the freezer for about 10 minutes.

2. Remove the chilled dough from the refrigerator or freezer. Use a 2.2-cm/0.9-in round pastry cutter to cut out about 10 to 15 small circular disks. Switch to a 5-cm/2-in round pastry cutter and cut out about 10 to 15 large disks from the dough. Return the cookie disks to the refrigerator or freezer until ready to use.

3. Follow the directions on page 12 to make the choux paste. Use ⅓ of the paste to make round mini choux and use the remaining ⅔ of the paste to make round large choux. Just before baking, place the crumble-cookie disks on top of the piped choux paste. Bake the choux according to the directions on pages 13 to 14 for mini and large choux.

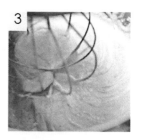

4. When the baked choux are completely cooled, use a 1-cm/0.38-in fine star tip (#864) to punch a hole in the bottom of each chou.

Pumpkin and Spice Mascarpone Cream:

1. In a medium-sized bowl, bloom the sheet gelatin in plenty of cold water. If powdered gelatin is used, sprinkle the powder over 20.4 g/0.72 oz cold water in the bowl. Let the gelatin bloom for at least 10 minutes before using.

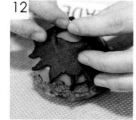

2. Combine the pumpkin puree, sugar, cinnamon powder, and nutmeg powder in a medium-sized stainless steel saucepan [1]. Mix well with a balloon whisk. Bring the mixture to 71°C/160°F over medium-high heat. Let cool slightly.

3. Meanwhile, squeeze excess water out of the bloomed sheet gelatin and add the gelatin to the pumpkin mixture [2]. If powdered gelatin is used, add the entire contents to the pumpkin mixture. Stir to combine. Cover the surface of the pumpkin jelly with plastic wrap. Let cool completely.

4. In a stand mixer fitted with a whisk attachment, whisk the mascarpone cheese until smooth. Gradually add the pumpkin jelly and whisk until the mixture is smooth and homogenous [3]. Chill the pumpkin-mascarpone cheese mixture in the refrigerator for 30 minutes to an hour.

5. In a stand mixer fitted with a whisk attachment, whisk the chilled heavy cream to medium peaks. Fold about ⅓ of the whipped cream into the pumpkin-mascarpone cheese mixture. Mix until well combined. Fold in the remaining whipped cream [4]. Reserve the filling in the refrigerator until ready to use.

Assembly and Decoration:

1. Fill a large pastry bag (45.7-cm/18-in) fitted with a 0.8-cm/0.31-in plain tip (#803) with the pumpkin-mascarpone cheese filling. Pipe the cream into each chou through the hole in the bottom.

2. To make the fondant glaze, in a medium-sized mixing bowl, combine the pastry fondant, 30° Baume syrup, and a few drops of orange gel food coloring. Gently heat the mixture over a double-boiler or in a microwave until the mixture reaches 37°C/99°F. Do not heat the mixture hotter than 50°C/122°F.

3. Dip the filled chou into the fondant glaze [5–7]. Gently shake off excess glaze and place the chou bottom-side down on a piece of parchment paper. Repeat until all the choux are glazed.

4. Take a large piece of marzipan and color it black. Take a piece of black marzipan, shape it into a ball, and then flatten it into a disk (about 7.6-cm/3-in in diameter). Trim both sides of the marzipan disk to shape it into a trapezoid.

5. Wrap the marzipan around your finger to shape it into a cone [8] and then close the seam and bend the top to shape the marzipan piece into a hat. Bend the bottom of the hat to make a rim; use a marzipan tool to make some creases [9].

6. Take another large piece of black marzipan and shape it into a trapezoid. Use a knife to make a few cuts on the longer edge [10]. Bend the marzipan into a cape [11]. Place the cape on top of a large chou [12] and then place a mini chou on the cape [13]. Finally, place the hat on top of the mini chou [14].

SANTA (CHESTNUTS)

Chestnuts always remind me of Christmas, partly because Nat King Cole's *Chestnuts Roasting on an Open Fire* is always playing on the radio during the Christmas season. One time I was grocery shopping in Austin, Texas, and that song was playing in the background. A woman approached me and said, "You know I really love this song, but I have no idea - what are chestnuts?" I was amused by her question since she was standing right in front of a pile of chestnuts on the produce shelf. I pointed behind her and she was mildly surprised and then turned around and asked me how to eat them. I explained to her that she can cut a cross on the end of the chestnuts, and then roast them, and no, it doesn't have to be roasted on an open fire. She smiled and thanked me. I love the aroma of roasting chestnuts, and I think this dessert can bring you that warm, toasty holiday atmosphere that we all love.

Yield: 15 individual pastries

Ingredients

Puff Pastry Base:

300 g/10.6 oz puff pastry dough (page 24)

Granulated sugar for dusting

Powdered sugar for dusting

Mini Choux:

100 g/3.5 oz crumble-cookie topping (page 16)

½ recipe (270 g/9.5 oz) pâte à choux (page 12)

Chestnut Cream:

120 g/4.2 oz pastry cream (page 17)

50 g/1.8 oz chestnut paste

8 g/0.28 oz (½ Tbsp) Cognac

80 g/2.8 oz unsalted butter, at room temperature

150 g/5.3 oz heavy whipping cream

20 g/0.71 oz granulated sugar

Puff Pastry Base:

1. Roll out the puff pastry dough (page 24) to about 3-mm/0.1-in thick. Allow the dough to rest in the refrigerator for 15 minutes. Dock the dough with a dough docker or fork. Cut the dough into 10-cm x 3.8-cm/4-in x 1.5-in rectangles.

2. Place the puff pastry rectangles on a half-sheet baking pan lined with a silicone baking mat or parchment paper [1]. Loosely cover the pan with plastic wrap and allow the dough to rest in the refrigerator for an hour.

3. Preheat the oven to 191°C/375°F. Sprinkle the puff pastry dough with granulated sugar [2]. To prevent the puff pastries from puffing up too much, place another piece of parchment paper or silicone mat on the dough and then place a cooling rack on top [3, 4].

4. Bake for about 25 minutes until the pastries are light golden brown. Remove the rack and silicone mat or parchment paper. Dust the puff pastries with powdered sugar [5].

5. Bake at 218°C/425°F for 3 to 5 minutes until the pastries are caramelized on top. Let cool completely before using.

Assembly and Decoration:

300 g/10.6 oz pastry fondant (page 21)

80 g/2.8 oz 30° Baume syrup (page 21)

Marzipan

Red gel food coloring

Granulated sugar

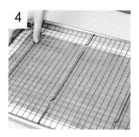

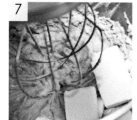

Mini Choux:

1. Follow the directions on page 16 to make the crumble-cookie topping. Roll out the dough between two pieces of parchment paper to 2-mm/0.08-in thick. Chill the dough in the refrigerator for about 45 minutes or in the freezer for about 10 minutes.

2. Remove the chilled dough from the refrigerator or freezer. Use a 2.2-cm/0.9-in round pastry cutter to cut out circular disks from the dough. Return the cookie disks to the refrigerator or freezer until ready to use.

3. Follow the directions on page 12 to make round mini choux. Just before baking, place the crumble-cookie disks on top of the piped choux paste. Bake the choux according to the directions on page 13.

4. When the baked choux are completely cooled, use a 0.8-cm/0.31-in fine star tip (#863) to punch a hole in the bottom of each chou.

Chestnut Cream:

1. Combine the pastry cream (page 17), chestnut paste, and Cognac in a mixer bowl. Beat with a stand mixer fitted with a wire whisk attachment on medium-high speed until the mixture is smooth [6].

2. Reduce the mixer speed to medium-low and whisk in the soft butter [7]. Once all the butter is incorporated, adjust the mixer to medium-high speed. Continue to beat for a few more minutes until the cream is light and fluffy [8].

3. Meanwhile, whisk the chilled heavy cream and sugar to medium-soft peaks. Gently fold about ½ of the whipped cream into the chestnut mixture. Mix until well combined. Fold in the remaining whipped cream. Reserve the filling in the refrigerator until ready to use.

Assembly and Decoration:

1. Fill a large pastry bag (45.7-cm/18-in) fitted with a 0.6-cm/0.25-in plain tip (#802) with the chestnut cream. Pipe the cream into each chou through the hole in the bottom.

2. To make the fondant glaze, in a medium-sized mixing bowl, combine the pastry fondant and 30° Baume syrup. Gently heat the mixture over a double-boiler or in a microwave until the mixture reaches 37°C/99°F. Do not heat the mixture hotter than 50°C/122°F.

3. Dip the filled chou into the fondant glaze [9]. Gently shake off excess glaze and place the chou bottom-side down on a piece of parchment paper. Repeat until all the choux are glazed.

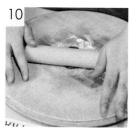

4. Take a large piece of marzipan and color it red. Take a medium-sized piece of red marzipan; shape it into a ball and then flatten it using a rolling pin [10]. Trim both sides of the marzipan disk to shape it into a trapezoid [11].

5. Wrap the marzipan around your finger to shape it into a cone [12] and then close the seam and bend the top to shape the marzipan piece into a hat.

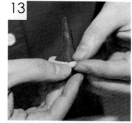

6. Take a small piece of natural-color marzipan and roll it into a log. Wrap the log around the bottom of the hat to make a rim [13]. Take another small piece of natural-color marzipan and shape it into a small ball. Attach the ball to the tip of the hat [14]. Dip the rim and tip portions of the hat into granulated sugar. Repeat to make more hats.

7. Place two filled choux on top of the puff pastry base [15, 16]. Place the marzipan hats on top of the filled choux [17].

THE SON OF CHOU
(GREEN APPLE MASCARPONE AND CARAMEL)

I spent most of my time during my college sophomore year in lecture halls, laboratories, and the library. My Thursday routine usually included attending engineering lectures and preparing the lab report. My favorite workspace was a small cubical in a quiet corner of the library next to the semiconductor book shelves. On one occasion, the engineering floor in the library was fully packed on a Thursday just before final exams. Naturally, my favorite workspace was occupied by a few students who were feverishly working on their project reports. Reluctantly, I had to search for a new spot in a different location in the library, and I ended up discovering a quiet corner in the modern art section. Soon I was captivated by the cover art of a book on the shelf right next to me; the cover had a painting of a man in a bowler hat with his face obscured by a green apple. I couldn't help myself from taking the book off the shelf and, almost instantly, I was mesmerized by its contents. The book was an introduction to surrealism and the cover painting was called *The Son of Man* by Belgian surrealist painter René Magritte. Soon I was in a world of Salvador Dalí, Joan Miró, and Max Ernst and surrounded by their dreamlike landscapes and subjects. On that day, I discovered my favorite art movement unexpectedly, not to mention my favorite workspace in the library. In this dessert, I try to capture the moment when I made that wonderful discovery during my college years.

Yield: about 10 individual pastries

INGREDIENTS

Mini and Large Choux:

200 g/7.1 oz crumble-cookie topping (page 16)

1 recipe pâte à choux (page 12)

Green Apple Mascarpone Cream:

4 g/0.14 oz gelatin sheet (silver grade) or 3.4 g/0.12 oz powdered gelatin + 20.4 g/0.72 oz cold water

170 g/6 oz green apple puree

45 g/1.6 oz granulated sugar

150 g/5.3 oz mascarpone cheese, at room temperature

150 g/5.3 oz heavy whipping cream

Mini and Large Choux:

1. Follow the directions on page 16 to make the crumble-cookie topping. Roll out the dough between two pieces of parchment paper to 2-mm/0.08-in thick. Chill the dough in the refrigerator for about 45 minutes or in the freezer for about 10 minutes.

2. Remove the chilled dough from the refrigerator or freezer. Use a 2.2-cm/0.9-in round pastry cutter to cut out about 10 to 15 small circular disks. Switch to a 5-cm/2-in round pastry cutter and cut out about 10 to 15 large disks from the dough. Return the cookie disks to the refrigerator or freezer until ready to use.

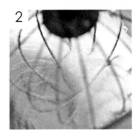

3. Follow the directions on page 12 to make the choux paste. Use ⅓ of the paste to make round mini choux and use the remaining ⅔ of the paste to make round large choux. Just before baking, place the crumble-cookie disks on top of the piped choux paste. Bake the choux according to the directions on pages 13 to 14 for mini and large choux.

Butter-Caramel:

100 g/3.5 oz heavy whipping cream

65 g/2.3 oz granulated sugar

1 g/0.035 oz (⅛ tsp) kosher salt or fine sea salt

60 g/2.1 oz unsalted butter, at room temperature

Assembly and Decoration:

300 g/10.6 oz pastry fondant (page 21)

80 g/2.8 oz 30° Baume syrup (page 21)

Green gel food coloring

Marzipan

Black gel food coloring

Red gel food coloring

4. When the baked choux are completely cooled, use a 1-cm/0.38-in fine star tip (#864) to punch a hole in the bottom of each chou.

Green Apple Mascarpone Cream:

1. In a medium-sized bowl, bloom the sheet gelatin in plenty of cold water. If powdered gelatin is used, sprinkle the powder over 20.4 g/0.72 oz cold water in the bowl. Let the gelatin bloom for at least 10 minutes before using.

2. Combine the green apple puree and sugar in a medium-sized stainless steel saucepan. Mix well with a balloon whisk. Bring the mixture to 71°C/160°F over medium-high heat. Let cool slightly.

3. Meanwhile, squeeze excess water out of the bloomed sheet gelatin and add the gelatin to the apple mixture [1]. If powdered gelatin is used, add the entire contents to the apple mixture. Stir to combine. Cover the surface of the apple jelly with plastic wrap. Let cool completely.

4. In a stand mixer fitted with a whisk attachment, whisk the mascarpone cheese until smooth. Gradually add the apple jelly and whisk until the mixture is smooth and homogenous [2]. Chill the apple-mascarpone cheese mixture in the refrigerator for 30 minutes to an hour.

5. In a stand mixer fitted with a whisk attachment, whisk the chilled heavy cream to medium peaks. Fold about ⅓ of the whipped cream into the apple-mascarpone cheese mixture. Mix until well combined. Fold in the remaining whipped cream [3]. Reserve the filling in the refrigerator until ready to use.

Butter-Caramel:

1. Place the heavy cream in a medium-sized stainless steel saucepan and set aside.

2. Place the sugar in a large stainless steel saucepan in an even layer. Dry melt the sugar over medium heat undisturbed for 3 to 5 minutes [4].

3. Meanwhile, heat the cream over high heat. Remove the pan from heat when the cream comes to a boil. Reserve.

4. When most of the sugar underneath the top layer of granules has melted and turned a golden color, reduce the heat to low. Stir occasionally with a spatula to avoid burning the caramel [5].

5. When all the sugar is melted and the caramel turns medium-dark amber at around 180°C/356°F, pour the hot cream into pan. Stir vigorously to smooth out any lumps [6].

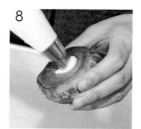

6. Continue to cook the caramel for another 2 to 3 minutes while stirring constantly. Cook until the caramel is smooth and velvety. Remove from heat and add salt and softened butter. Stir until the mixture is smooth and homogenous.

7. Let the butter-caramel cool slightly. Cover the surface of the caramel with plastic wrap. Allow the butter-caramel to cool completely before using.

Assembly and Decoration:

1. Fill a large pastry bag (45.7-cm/18-in) fitted with a 0.8-cm/0.31-in plain tip (#803) with the butter-caramel. Pipe a small amount of butter-caramel into each large chou [7]. Fill another large pastry bag (45.7-cm/18-in) fitted with a 0.8-cm/0.31-in plain tip (#803) with the apple-mascarpone cheese filling. Pipe more apple-mascarpone cream into each large chou [8].

2. Pipe a small amount of the remaining apple-mascarpone cream into each mini chou through the hole in the bottom.

3. To make the fondant glaze, in a medium-sized mixing bowl, combine the pastry fondant and 30° Baume syrup. Gently heat the mixture over a double-boiler or in a microwave until the mixture reaches 37°C/99°F. Do not heat the mixture hotter than 50°C/122°F.

4. Place about ⅓ of the fondant in a medium-sized bowl and add a few drops of green food coloring. Dip the filled mini chou into the green fondant glaze [9]. Gently shake off excess glaze and place the chou bottom-side down on a piece of parchment paper.

5. Dip the filled large chou into the remaining white fondant glaze [10]. Gently shake off excess glaze and place the chou bottom-side down on a piece of parchment paper. Repeat until all the choux are glazed.

6. Take three large pieces of marzipan and color them black, red, and green. Take a piece of black marzipan, shape it into a ball, and then flatten it. Use a pastry cutter to cut out a disk (about 3.8-cm/1.5-in in diameter) [11]. Take another piece of black marzipan and shape it into the top portion of the hat. Attach it to the bottom disk and bend the rim so that it resembles a bowler hat [12].

7. Take a piece of red marzipan and flatten it. Use a knife to cut it into a tie shape [13].

8. Take two small pieces of green marzipan and shape them into leaves [14]. Attach the leaves on the rim of the bowler hat.

9. Place the tie on a large chou [15] and then place a mini chou on top of the tie. Finally, place the bowler hat on top of the mini chou [16].

WILD WEST (RED BEAN PASTE)

My family relocated from Connecticut to Texas when I was in high school. For the first time, I saw the real Wild West. In the first summer after we arrived in Texas, my mother and I decided to take a road trip out west. The two of us drove for days from Texas all the way to Yellowstone National Park in Wyoming. On our way back home, we took a different route through Grand Canyon National Park in Arizona. Witnessing the true grandeur of the American wildness for the first time, my heart was filled with excitement and a sense of adventure during the entire trip. My mother and I took turns driving. I had received my driver's license two months prior to our trip and I had a tendency to drive faster when I was nervous. On one morning, I zoomed through Rocky Mountain hairpin turns at Grand Prix speed with sheer-drop cliffs hanging outside the passenger window. To this day, my mother recalls that as one of the scariest days in her life. Not surprisingly, we saw some real-life cowboys on our journey west, and what is the most common food cowboys like? Beans, of course! I created this dessert to reminisce about our first Wild West encounters. Note that you can find ready-made sweet bean paste at most Asian grocers.

Yield: about 10 individual pastries

Ingredients

Mini and Large Choux:

200 g/7.1 oz crumble-cookie topping (page 16)

1 recipe pâte à choux (page 12)

Red Bean Diplomat Cream:

200 g/7.1 oz sweetened fine red bean paste

200 g/7.1 oz pastry cream (page 17)

0.5 g/0.018 oz (¼ tsp) cinnamon powder

0.5 g/0.018 oz (¼ tsp) allspice powder

200 g/7.1 oz heavy whipping cream

Assembly and Decoration:

Chocolate glaze (page 20)

Marzipan

Red gel food coloring

Brown gel food coloring

Mini and Large Choux:

1. Follow the directions on page 16 to make the crumble-cookie topping.

2. Roll out the dough between two pieces of parchment paper to 2-mm/0.08-in thick. Chill the dough in the refrigerator for about 45 minutes or in the freezer for about 10 minutes.

3. Remove the chilled dough from the refrigerator or freezer. Use a 2.2-cm/0.9-in round pastry cutter to cut out about 10 to 15 small circular disks. Switch to a 5-cm/2-in round pastry cutter and cut out about 10 to 15 large disks from the dough. Return the cookie disks to the refrigerator or freezer until ready to use.

4. Follow the directions on page 12 to make the choux paste. Use ⅓ of the paste to make round mini choux and use the remaining ⅔ of the paste to make round large choux. Just before baking, place the crumble-cookie disks on top of the piped choux paste. Bake the choux according to the directions on pages 13 to 14 for mini and large choux.

5. When the baked choux are completely cooled, use a 1-cm/0.38-in fine star tip (#864) to punch a hole in the bottom of each chou.

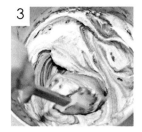

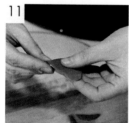

Red Bean Diplomat Cream:

1. Combine the red bean paste, pastry cream, cinnamon powder, and allspice powder in a mixer bowl [1]. Attach the bowl to a stand mixer fitted with a whisk attachment. Whisk the mixture on high speed until it is light and smooth [2].

2. Meanwhile, whisk the chilled heavy cream to medium peaks. Fold about ⅓ of the whipped cream into the red bean mixture. Mix until well combined. Fold in the remaining whipped cream [3]. Reserve the filling in the refrigerator until ready to use.

Assembly and Decoration:

1. Fill a large pastry bag (45.7-cm/18-in) fitted with a 0.8-cm/0.31-in plain tip (#803) with the red bean diplomat cream. Pipe the cream into each chou through the hole in the bottom.

2. Gently heat the chocolate glaze in a microwave at 10-second increments and stir the glaze after each heating. Take care not to over-heat the glaze. Use the glaze at 25°C/77°F.

3. Dip the filled chou into the chocolate glaze [4, 5]. Gently shake off excess glaze and place the chou bottom-side down on a piece of parchment paper. Repeat until all the choux are glazed.

4. Take two large pieces of marzipan and color them red and brown. Take a piece of brown marzipan, shape it into a ball, and then flatten it using a rolling pin [6]. Use a pastry cutter to cut out a disk (about 5-cm/2-in in diameter) [7]. Take another piece of brown marzipan and shape it into the top portion of the hat [8, 9]. Attach it to the bottom disk and bend the rim so that it resembles a cowboy hat [10].

5. Take a piece of red marzipan and shape it into a triangle to make the bandana [11]. Place the bandana on top of a large chou [12] and then place a mini chou on the bandana. Finally, place the cowboy hat on top of the mini chou [13].

SAVORY

GOUGÈRES

When I think of savory choux pastry, the classic gougère is the first thing that comes to my mind. Simply adding grated gruyère cheese to the choux paste and perhaps a savory touch for the topping makes this a crowd pleaser for any gathering.

Yield: about 60 3.8-cm/1.5-in gougères

INGREDIENTS

120 g/4.2 oz all-purpose flour

100 g/3.5 oz distilled water

100 g/3.5 oz whole milk

4 g/0.14 oz (½ tsp) kosher salt or fine sea salt

80 g/2.8 oz unsalted butter

200 g/7.1 oz whole eggs

20 g/0.71 oz egg whites

80 g/2.8 oz gruyère cheese, finely grated

1 whole egg for egg wash

Freshly ground black pepper

40 g/1.4 oz gruyère cheese or parmesan cheese, finely grated

1. Sift the flour onto a piece of parchment paper. Transfer the sifted flour to a bowl and reserve.

2. Combine the water, milk, salt, and butter in a large stainless steel saucepan; heat the mixture over medium-high heat.

3. When the mixture comes to a boil, remove the saucepan from heat. Carefully whisk the sifted flour into the mixture. When all of the flour is incorporated into the liquid, shake off lumps of dough from the whisk and switch to a spatula or wooden spoon.

4. Return the saucepan to medium-low heat. Continue to cook for 2 to 3 minutes; stir constantly, using a folding motion to eliminate any remaining small lumps of flour and bring the dough pieces together. Cook until a smooth and thick paste is obtained.

5. Transfer the dough to a mixer bowl. Attach the bowl to a mixer fitted with a paddle attachment. Mix the dough at medium speed for 10 to 15 seconds to release the steam.

6. Add the eggs one at a time while continuing to mix on medium speed. Make sure each egg is incorporated before adding additional eggs. Add the egg whites. Scrape down the sides of the mixer bowl with a spatula if necessary. Increase the mixer speed to high. Mix for 10 to 20 seconds or until a smooth paste forms. Fold in the grated gruyère cheese (80 g/2.8 oz) [1].

7. Meanwhile, line a half-sheet baking pan with a silicone baking mat or parchment paper. Preheat the oven to 191°C/375°F. Fill a large pastry bag (45.7-cm/18-in) fitted with a 1.3-cm/0.5-in plain tip (#806) with the choux paste. Pipe the paste into 2.5-cm/1-in mounds with 2.5-cm/1-in spacing on the baking mat or parchment paper. Brush the top with egg wash using a gentle dabbing motion.

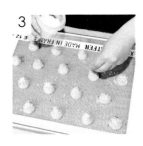

8. Sprinkle ground black pepper and grated gruyère or parmesan cheese on top [2, 3]. Bake at 191°C/375°F for about 16 minutes until the choux are puffed up. Reduce the temperature to 177°C/350°F and bake for another 8 minutes until the choux are golden brown. Turn off the oven and leave the choux in the oven undisturbed for another 6 minutes. Remove the baked choux from the oven and serve warm [4].

SMOKED SALMON

This savory pastry combines the best of two worlds! The buttery and flaky puff pastry on the bottom is transformed into an airy, crunchy chou on top that is filled with a delightful salmon mousse. Although it is a bit involved to make two types of pastry dough, I think it is well worth the effort once you have tried this remarkable pastry.

Yield: about 15 to 20 round savory pastries

INGREDIENTS

Puff Pastry Base with Choux:

300 g/10.6 oz puff pastry dough (page 24)

90 g/3.2 oz all-purpose flour

75 g/2.6 oz distilled water

75 g/2.6 oz whole milk

3 g/0.11 oz (⅜ tsp) kosher salt or fine sea salt

60 g/2.1 oz unsalted butter

150 g/5.3 oz whole eggs

1 whole egg for egg wash

Salmon Mousse:

150 g/5.3 oz smoked salmon

80 g/2.8 oz distilled water, chilled

6 g/0.21 oz (2 Tbsp) fresh dill, chopped

15 g/0.53 oz (1 Tbsp) Pernod

20 g/0.71 oz (1 Tbsp) honey

2 g/0.071 oz (¼ tsp) kosher salt or fine sea salt

1 g/0.035 oz (¼ tsp) freshly ground black pepper

Puff Pastry Base with Choux:

1. Roll out the puff pastry dough (page 24) to about 3-mm/0.1-in thick. Allow the dough to rest in the refrigerator for 15 minutes. Dock the dough with a dough docker or fork [1]. Use a 5-cm/2-in round pastry cutter to cut out disks from the dough [2].

2. Place the puff pastry disks on a half-sheet baking pan lined with a silicone baking mat or parchment paper. Loosely cover the pan with plastic wrap and allow the dough to rest in the refrigerator for an hour.

3. For the savory choux, sift the flour onto a piece of parchment paper. Transfer the sifted flour to a bowl and reserve.

4. Combine the water, milk, salt, and butter in a large stainless steel saucepan; heat the mixture over medium-high heat.

5. When the mixture comes to a boil, remove the saucepan from heat. Carefully whisk the sifted flour into the mixture. When all the flour is incorporated into the liquid, shake off lumps of dough from the whisk and switch to a spatula or wooden spoon.

6. Return the saucepan to medium-low heat. Continue to cook for 2 to 3 minutes; stir constantly, using a folding motion to eliminate any remaining small lumps of flour and bring the dough pieces together. Cook until a smooth and thick paste is obtained.

200 g/7.1 oz heavy whipping cream

Assembly and Decoration:

Smoked salmon, coarsely chopped

Fresh dill

7. Transfer the dough to a mixer bowl. Attach the bowl to a mixer fitted with a paddle attachment. Mix the dough at medium speed for 10 to 15 seconds to release the steam.

8. Add the eggs one at a time while continuing to mix on medium speed. Make sure each egg is incorporated before adding additional eggs. Scrape down the sides of the mixer bowl with a spatula if necessary. Increase the mixer speed to high. Mix for 10 to 20 seconds or until a smooth paste forms.

9. Preheat the oven to 191°C/375°F. Fill a large pastry bag (45.7-cm/18-in) fitted with a 1.7-cm/0.69-in plain tip (#809) with the choux paste. Remove the chilled puff pastry disks from the refrigerator. Pipe the choux paste into 3.8-cm/1.5-in mounds on top of the puff pastry disks [3]. Lightly brush the pastries with egg wash [4].

10. Bake at 191°C/375°F for about 18 minutes until the puff pastry-choux are puffed up. Reduce the temperature to 177°C/350°F and bake for another 15 minutes until the pastries are golden brown. Turn off the oven and leave the pastries in the oven undisturbed for another 10 minutes. Remove the baked pastries from the oven and let cool completely [5].

Salmon Mousse:

1. In a food processor or blender, combine all ingredients for the salmon mousse except for the cream. Blend the mixture until smooth and well combined [6].

2. Whip the chilled heavy cream to medium-soft peaks. Gently fold about half of the whipped cream into the salmon mixture; fold until the mixture is homogenous. Fold in the remaining whipped cream [7]. Reserve the salmon mousse in the refrigerator until ready to use.

Assembly and Decoration:

1. Using a serrated knife, cut off the top ⅓ of each puff pastry-chou [8] and reserve the cap.

2. Fill a large pastry bag (45.7-cm/18-in) fitted with a 1.3-cm/0.5-in plain tip (#806) with the salmon mousse. Pipe the salmon mousse into the puff pastry-chou [9]. Garnish the top with smoked salmon pieces and fresh dill [10]. Place the reserved cap on top. Repeat to finish assembling all pastries.

SHRIMP CHOUX

One time I was driving from Atlanta to Houston to visit my parents; a fuel truck was overturned on the highway when I was in southern Louisiana. Reluctantly I was rerouted to local roads. After 20 minutes' driving, I found myself lost in the backwoods surrounded by swampland. It was getting dark; the eerie shadows cast by the tupelo trees in the murky water made me feel particularly uneasy. I felt like I was being watched by creatures in the marsh. Finally, a rundown shack appeared on my horizon; a hand-painted, slightly crooked sign that said "Seafood, Po'boy" was hanging on the door. I hesitated to go inside; after all, it was the perfect setting for a horror movie. But I was tired, hungry, and hopelessly lost, plus the upbeat zydeco music that was play-ing sounded welcoming. I went inside and ordered a fried seafood platter. The portion was huge; there were some easily recognizable items such as fried catfish, crawfish, and some excellent fried shrimp and shrimp croquettes. But there were also some mystery items on the plate; although they were delicious, I had no clue what they were. Later on, I found out they were fried frog legs and alligator tail meat. Well, it was definitely a memorable day. I was glad that I had some alligator meat for the first time, and not the other way around.

The fried shrimp and croquettes inspired me to create this savory appetizer. You can use shrimp without head on in this recipe, but I think the head-on shrimp create a more stunning presentation. Better yet, if you prefer, alligator tails and frog legs will work in this recipe too!

Yield: about 50 shrimp choux

Ingredients

120 g/4.2 oz all-purpose flour

190 g/6.7 oz distilled water

80 g/2.8 oz extra-virgin olive oil

4 g/0.14 oz (½ tsp) kosher salt or fine sea salt

0.5 g/0.018 oz (¼ tsp) cayenne pepper

200 g/7.1 oz whole eggs

40 g/1.4 oz egg whites

910 g/2 lb large head-on in-shell shrimp

Oil for frying

1. Sift the flour onto a piece of parchment paper. Transfer the sifted flour to a bowl and reserve.

2. Combine the water, olive oil, salt, and cayenne pepper in a large stainless steel saucepan; heat the mixture over medium-high heat.

3. When the mixture comes to a boil [1], remove the saucepan from heat. Carefully whisk the sift-ed flour into the mixture [2]. When all the flour is incorporated into the liquid, shake off lumps of dough from the whisk and switch to a spatula or wooden spoon.

4. Return the saucepan to medium-low heat. Con-tinue to cook for 2 to 3 minutes; stir constantly, us-ing a folding motion to eliminate any remaining small lumps of flour and bring the dough pieces together. Cook until a smooth and thick paste is obtained [3].

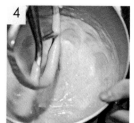

5. Transfer the dough to a mixer bowl. Attach the bowl to a mixer fitted with a paddle attachment. Mix the dough at medium speed for 10 to 15 seconds to release the steam.

6. Add the whole eggs one at a time while continuing to mix on medium speed. Make sure each egg is incorporated before adding additional eggs. Add the egg whites. Scrape down the sides of the mixer bowl with a spatula if necessary. Increase the mixer speed to high. Mix for 10 to 20 seconds or until a smooth batter forms [4].

7. Cover the surface of the batter with plastic wrap. Chill in the refrigerator for 30 minutes before using.

8. Meanwhile, remove the shells from the mid-section of the shrimp, but keep the shell intact for the tail. Keep the head on as well [5].

9. Cut along the back side of the shrimp's mid-section and devein the shrimp. Cut a small slit in the shrimp's mid-section near the head [6]. Bend the shrimp following its natural curve and insert the tail into the slit [7, 8]. Repeat to finish preparing all the shrimp.

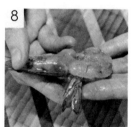

10. Meanwhile, heat the oil in a Dutch oven or a deep fryer to 177°C/350°F. Remove the chilled choux batter from the refrigerator. Hold the head and tail of the shrimp and dip it into the batter [9]. Carefully drop the batter-coated shrimp into the hot oil [10]. Fry for 2 to 3 minutes until the shrimp turn golden brown [11, 12]. Serve immediately.

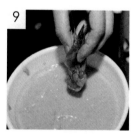

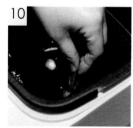

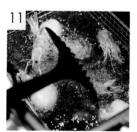

SMOKED CRAB AND MANGO SALAD

A complete flavor explosion in a bite, this crab salad has sweetness from the mangoes, smokiness from the roasted peppers and apple wood smoke, tenderness from the crab meat, and acidity from the vinaigrette. The puff pastry with choux are the perfect serving vessels for this delectable salad.

Yield: about 24 round savory pastries

INGREDIENTS

Puff Pastry Base with Choux:

500 g/17.6 oz puff pastry dough (page 24)

90 g/3.2 oz all-purpose flour

75 g/2.6 oz distilled water

75 g/2.6 oz whole milk

3 g/0.11 oz (⅜ tsp) kosher salt or fine sea salt

60 g/2.1 oz unsalted butter

150 g/5.3 oz whole eggs

1 whole egg for egg wash

Smoked Crab Salad:

250 g/8.8 oz jumbo lump crab meat

Apple wood chips for smoking

30 g/1.1 oz (2 Tbsp) extra-virgin olive oil

2.5 g/0.088 oz (1 tsp) minced garlic

7.5 g/0.26 oz (1 Tbsp) minced shallot

2.5 g/0.088 oz (1 Tbsp) minced cilantro leaves

23 g/0.81 oz (1½ Tbsp) white wine vinegar

150 g/5.3 oz fresh mango, diced

Puff Pastry Base with Choux:

1. Roll out the puff pastry dough (page 24) to about 3-mm/0.1-in thick. Allow the dough to rest in the refrigerator for 15 minutes. Dock the dough with a dough docker or fork [1]. Use a 5-cm/2-in round pastry cutter to cut out disks from the dough [2].

2. Place the puff pastry disks on a half-sheet baking pan lined with a silicone baking mat or parchment paper. Loosely cover the pan with plastic wrap and allow the dough to rest in the refrigerator for an hour.

3. For the savory choux, sift the flour onto a piece of parchment paper. Transfer the sifted flour to a bowl and reserve.

4. Combine the water, milk, salt, and butter in a large stainless steel saucepan; heat the mixture over medium-high heat.

5. When the mixture comes to a boil, remove the saucepan from heat. Carefully whisk the sifted flour into the mixture. When all the flour is incorporated into the liquid, shake off lumps of dough from the whisk and switch to a spatula or wooden spoon.

6. Return the saucepan to medium-low heat. Continue to cook for 2 to 3 minutes; stir constantly, using a folding motion to eliminate any remaining small lumps of flour and bring the dough pieces together. Cook until a smooth and thick paste is obtained.

100 g/3.5 oz roasted red pepper, diced

Special Equipment:

Smoking gun

7. Transfer the dough to a mixer bowl. Attach the bowl to a mixer fitted with a paddle attachment. Mix the dough at medium speed for 10 to 15 seconds to release the steam.

8. Add the eggs one at a time while continuing to mix on medium speed. Make sure each egg is incorporated before adding additional eggs. Scrape down the sides of the mixer bowl with a spatula if necessary. Increase the mixer speed to high. Mix for 10 to 20 seconds or until a smooth paste forms.

9. Preheat the oven to 191°C/375°F. Fill a large pastry bag (45.7-cm/18-in) fitted with a 0.8-cm/0.31-in plain tip (#803) with the choux paste. Remove the chilled puff pastry disks from the refrigerator. Pipe the choux paste along the outer edge of the puff pastry disks [3]. Lightly brush the pastries with egg wash [4].

10. Bake the puff pastry-choux at 191°C/375°F for about 23 minutes until they puff up and turn golden brown [5]. Let cool completely.

Smoked Crab Salad:

1. Place the jumbo lump crab meat in a medium-sized stainless steel mixing bowl; partially cover the bowl with plastic wrap. Reserve.

2. Insert the apple wood chips into the wood chip compartment of the smoking gun. Turn on the device and ignite the wood chips [6]. Insert the smoke-feeding tube into the mixing bowl with the crab meat [7, 8].

3. The mixing bowl should be filled with smoke after 10 to 20 seconds. Turn off the device. Immediately cover the mixing bowl tightly with plastic wrap.

4. Allow the crab meat to infuse for a few minutes and remove the plastic wrap [9]. Add the remaining ingredients for the crab salad to the mixing bowl. Carefully toss all ingredients until well combined [10]. Spoon the crab salad into the puff pastry-choux [11, 12] and serve immediately.

CHOU MARGHERITA

As its name suggests, this savory creation is inspired by the Neapolitan speciality—pizza Margherita. Like its counterpart, the chou Margherita contains similar ingredients, including buffalo mozzarella, tomatoes, basil, and olive oil, which complete the pizza flavor profile.

Yield: about 18 6.4-cm/2.5-in round savory pastries

INGREDIENTS

Olive Oil Choux:

120 g/4.2 oz all-purpose flour

185 g/6.5 oz distilled water

80 g/2.8 oz extra-virgin olive oil

4 g/0.14 oz (½ tsp) kosher salt or fine sea salt

200 g/7.1 oz whole eggs

1 whole egg for egg wash

40 g/1.4 oz parmesan cheese, finely grated

Tomato and Basil Jelly:

10 g/0.35 oz gelatin sheet (silver grade) or 8.4 g/0.3 oz powdered gelatin + 50.4 g/1.8 oz cold water

400 g/14.1 oz fresh tomato juice made from about 910 g/2 lb tomatoes

2 g/0.071 oz (¼ tsp) kosher salt or fine sea salt

6 g/0.21 oz (¼ cup) fresh basil leaves

Buffalo Mozzarella Mousse

200 g/7.1 oz fresh buffalo mozzarella

30 g/1.1 oz buffalo mozzarella brine

Olive Oil Choux:

1. Sift the flour onto a piece of parchment paper. Transfer the sifted flour to a bowl and reserve.

2. Combine the water, olive oil, and salt in a large stainless steel saucepan; heat the mixture over medium-high heat.

3. When the mixture comes to a boil [1], remove the saucepan from heat. Carefully whisk the sifted flour into the mixture [2]. When all the flour is incorporated into the liquid, shake off lumps of dough from the whisk and switch to a spatula or wooden spoon.

4. Return the saucepan to medium-low heat. Continue to cook for 2 to 3 minutes; stir constantly, using a folding motion to eliminate any remaining small lumps of flour and bring the dough pieces together. Cook until a smooth and thick paste is obtained [3].

5. Transfer the dough to a mixer bowl. Attach the bowl to a mixer fitted with a paddle attachment. Mix the dough at medium speed for 10 to 15 seconds to release the steam.

6. Add the eggs one at a time while continuing to mix on medium speed. Make sure each egg is incorporated before adding additional eggs. Scrape down the sides of the mixer bowl with a spatula if necessary. Increase the mixer speed to high. Mix for 10 to 20 seconds or until a smooth paste forms [4].

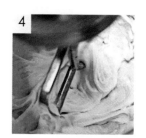

2 g/0.071 oz (¼ tsp) kosher salt or fine sea salt

200 g/7.1 oz heavy whipping cream

Assembly and Decoration:

100 g/3.5 oz parmesan cheese, finely grated

7. Meanwhile, line a half-sheet baking pan with a silicone baking mat or parchment paper. Preheat the oven to 191°C/375°F. Fill a large pastry bag (45.7-cm/18-in) fitted with a 1.7-cm/0.69-in plain tip (#809) with the choux paste. Pipe the paste into 5-cm/2-in mounds with 2.5-cm/1-in spacing on the baking mat or parchment paper [5]. Brush the top with egg wash using a gentle dabbing motion [6].

8. Bake at 191°C/375°F for about 20 minutes until the choux are puffed up. Reduce the temperature to 177°C/350°F and bake for another 15 minutes until the choux are golden brown. Turn off the oven and leave the choux in the oven undisturbed for another 10 minutes. Remove the baked choux from the oven [7].

9. Turn on the oven broiler; sprinkle parmesan cheese on top of the baked choux [8]. Place the baking pan under the broiler for 1 to 2 minutes until the cheese melts. Remove the baked choux from the oven and let cool completely [9].

Tomato and Basil Jelly:

1. In a medium-sized bowl, bloom the sheet gelatin in plenty of cold water. If powdered gelatin is used, sprinkle the powder over 50.4 g/1.8 oz cold water in the bowl. Let the gelatin bloom for at least 10 minutes before using.

2. To make fresh tomato juice, cut a shallow cross on the bottom of the tomatoes. Blanch the tomatoes in hot water for a few minutes until the skin starts to peel off.

3. Remove the tomato skins and stem ends. Sprinkle the peeled tomatoes with salt. Wait a few minutes. Crush the tomatoes using a masher. Strain the juice through a sieve into a mixing bowl. Let the tomato juice rest for 30 minutes. Then carefully pour the clear tomato juice into another bowl and discard the sediments on the bottom of the bowl.

4. Place 400 g/14.1 oz tomato juice in a medium-sized stainless steel saucepan. Bring the mixture to 71°C/160°F over medium-high heat. Let cool slightly.

5. Meanwhile, squeeze excess water out of the bloomed sheet gelatin and add the gelatin to the tomato juice [10]. If powdered gelatin is used, add the entire contents to the tomato juice. Stir to combine. Tear the fresh basil leaves into small pieces and add them to the tomato mixture [11].

6. Pour the mixture into a container with a flat bottom. Cover the surface of the tomato and basil jelly with plastic wrap. Chill in the refrigerator for about 2 hours.

Buffalo Mozzarella Mousse:

1. In a food processor or blender, combine all ingredients for the buffalo mozzarella mousse except for the cream [12]. Blend the mixture until it is smooth and well combined [13].

2. Whip the chilled heavy cream to stiff peaks. Gently fold about ½ of the whipped cream into the mozzarella mixture; fold until the mixture is homogenous. Fold in the remaining whipped cream [14]. Reserve the mozzarella mousse in the refrigerator until ready to use.

Assembly and Decoration:

1. To make parmesan cheese crackers, sprinkle the cheese on a baking pan lined with a silicone baking mat or parchment paper. Place the pan under the broiler for 2 to 3 minutes until the cheese melts. Let cool completely and break the cracker into small pieces.

2. Using a serrated knife, cut off the top ⅓ of each chou horizontally and reserve the cap [15].

3. Cut the tomato and basil jelly into small dices and fill the bottom of the chou with the jelly [16].

4. Fill a large pastry bag (45.7-cm/18-in) fitted with a 1-cm/0.38-in plain tip (#804) with the buffalo mozzarella mousse. Pipe the buffalo mozzarella mousse on top [17]. Add more tomato and basil jelly on top of the mousse [18].

5. Decorate the pastry with parmesan crackers; place the reserved cap on top.

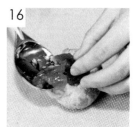

AVOCADO AND BACON

I think avocado is a strange fruit. It is not sweet, it does not have a distinct flavor, it has a squashy texture, and it is usually served in savory dishes but it is not a vegetable. It is a real oddball in the fruit family, and most people either love it or hate it. I love avocado! It is rich, creamy, and when it is paired with the right ingredients, it is absolutely addictive. I think bacon is one of those ingredients that complement avocados extremely well.

Yield: about 30 7.5-cm/3-in éclairs

INGREDIENTS

Savory Éclairs:

120 g/4.2 oz all-purpose flour

100 g/3.5 oz distilled water

100 g/3.5 oz whole milk

4 g/0.14 oz (½ tsp) kosher salt or fine sea salt

80 g/2.8 oz unsalted butter

200 g/7.1 oz whole eggs

1 whole egg for egg wash

Avocado Mousse:

400 g/14.1 oz ripe avocado flesh

30 g/1.1 oz (2 Tbsp) lime juice

4 g/0.14 oz (1 Tbsp) lime zest

2.5 g/0.088 oz (1 tsp) minced garlic

10 g/0.35 oz (2 Tbsp) green onion, chopped

5 g/0.18 oz (1 tsp) green Tabasco sauce

2.5 g/0.088 oz (1 Tbsp) cilantro leaves

100 g/3.5 oz mascarpone cheese

4 g/0.14 oz (½ tsp) kosher salt or fine sea salt

Savory Éclairs:

1. Sift the flour onto a piece of parchment paper. Transfer the sifted flour to a bowl and reserve.

2. Combine the water, milk, salt, and butter in a large stainless steel saucepan; heat the mixture over medium-high heat.

3. When the mixture comes to a boil, remove the saucepan from heat. Carefully whisk the sifted flour into the mixture. When all the flour is incorporated into the liquid, shake off lumps of dough from the whisk and switch to a spatula or wooden spoon.

4. Return the saucepan to medium-low heat. Continue to cook for 2 to 3 minutes; stir constantly, using a folding motion to eliminate any remaining small lumps of flour and bring the dough pieces together. Cook until a smooth and thick paste is obtained.

5. Transfer the dough to a mixer bowl. Attach the bowl to a mixer fitted with a paddle attachment. Mix the dough at medium speed for 10 to 15 seconds to release the steam.

6. Add the eggs one at a time while continuing to mix on medium speed. Make sure each egg is incorporated before adding additional eggs. Scrape down the sides of the mixer bowl with a spatula if necessary. Increase the mixer speed to high. Mix for 10 to 20 seconds or until a smooth paste forms.

7. Meanwhile, line a half-sheet baking pan with a silicone baking mat or parchment paper. Preheat

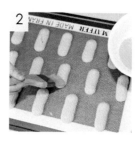

1 g/0.035 oz (¼ tsp) freshly ground black pepper

100 g/3.5 oz heavy whipping cream

Assembly and Decoration:

50 g/1.8 oz cooked bacon, diced

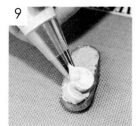

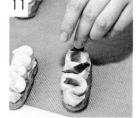

the oven to 191°C/375°F. Fill a large pastry bag (45.7-cm/18-in) fitted with a 1.3-cm/0.5-in fine star tip (#866) with the choux paste. Pipe the paste into 7.5-cm/3-in logs with 2.5-cm/1-in spacing on the baking mat or parchment paper [1]. Brush the top with egg wash using a gentle dabbing motion [2].

8. Bake at 191°C/375°F for about 15 minutes until the éclairs are puffed up. Reduce the temperature to 177°C/350°F and bake for another 15 minutes until the éclairs are golden brown. Turn off the oven and leave the éclairs in the oven undisturbed for another 10 minutes. Remove the baked éclairs from the oven and let cool completely [3].

Avocado Mousse:

1. In a food processor or blender, combine all ingredients for the avocado mousse except for the cream [4]. Blend the mixture until it is smooth and well combined [5].

2. Whip the chilled heavy cream to stiff peaks. Gently fold about ½ of the whipped cream into the avocado mixture; fold until the mixture is homogenous. Fold in the remaining whipped cream [6]. Reserve the avocado mousse in the refrigerator until ready to use.

Assembly and Decoration:

1. Using a serrated knife, cut off the top ⅓ of each éclair horizontally [7].

2. Fill the bottom of the éclair with the avocado mousse. Use an offset spatula to level the mousse [8].

3. Fill a large pastry bag (45.7-cm/18-in) fitted with a small St. Honoré tip (2-cm/0.8-in opening) with the remaining avocado mousse. Pipe more avocado mousse on top in a zigzag pattern [9, 10].

4. Place cooked bacon pieces on top [11].

TUNA AND SESAME

This pastry is inspired by my favorite appetizer—seared tuna with sesame seeds. The choux are made with sesame oil and sesame seeds to capture the theme of the original dish. I use the marinating ingredients for the tuna to create the soy and ginger mousse. Whether served with or without the seared tuna, the sesame choux are delicious! They can be an interesting and unusual addition to any ensemble of appetizers.

Yield: about 20 kabobs

Ingredients

Sesame Choux:

120 g/4.2 oz all-purpose flour

180 g/6.3 oz distilled water

80 g/2.8 oz untoasted sesame oil

4 g/0.14 oz (½ tsp) kosher salt or fine sea salt

200 g/7.1 oz whole eggs

1 whole egg for egg wash

Mixed-color sesame seeds for coating

Soy and Ginger Mousse:

15 g/0.53 oz (1 Tbsp) soy sauce

30 g/1.1 oz (2 Tbsp) pickled ginger brine

15 g/0.53 oz (1 Tbsp) fresh orange juice

20 g/0.71 oz (1 Tbsp) honey

8 g/0.28 oz (1 tsp) wasabi paste

2 g/0.071 oz (¼ tsp) kosher salt or fine sea salt

200 g/7.1 oz heavy whipping cream

Seared Ahi Tuna:

250 g/8.8 oz Ahi tuna steak

Sesame Choux:

1. Sift the flour onto a piece of parchment paper. Transfer the sifted flour to a bowl and reserve.

2. Combine the water, sesame oil, and salt in a large stainless steel saucepan; heat the mixture over medium-high heat.

3. When the mixture comes to a boil [1], remove the saucepan from heat. Carefully whisk the sifted flour into the mixture [2]. When all the flour is incorporated into the liquid, shake off lumps of dough from the whisk and switch to a spatula or wooden spoon.

4. Return the saucepan to medium-low heat. Continue to cook for 2 to 3 minutes; stir constantly, using a folding motion to eliminate any remaining small lumps of flour and bring the dough pieces together. Cook until a smooth and thick paste is obtained [3].

5. Transfer the dough to a mixer bowl. Attach the bowl to a mixer fitted with a paddle attachment. Mix the dough at medium speed for 10 to 15 seconds to release the steam.

6. Add the eggs one at a time while continuing to mix on medium speed [4]. Make sure each egg is incorporated before adding additional eggs. Scrape down the sides of the mixer bowl with a spatula if necessary. Increase the mixer speed to high. Mix for 10 to 20 seconds or until a smooth paste forms [5].

15 g/0.53 oz (1 Tbsp) soy sauce

10 g/0.35 oz (2 Tbsp) fresh ginger, coarsely chopped

20 g/0.71 oz (1 Tbsp) honey

4 g/0.14 oz (½ tsp) wasabi paste

8 g/0.28 oz (½ Tbsp) sesame oil

1 g/0.035 oz (1 tsp) freshly grated orange zest

Mixed-color sesame seeds for coating

Oil for cooking

Assembly and Decoration:

Siphon whip with injector attachment

N₂O siphon whip charger

Bamboo skewers

7. Meanwhile, line a half-sheet baking pan with a silicone baking mat or parchment paper. Preheat the oven to 191°C/375°F. Fill a large pastry bag (45.7-cm/18-in) fitted with a 1.3-cm/0.5-in plain tip (#806) with the choux paste. Pipe the paste into 2-cm/0.8-in mounds with 2.5-cm/1-in spacing on the baking mat or parchment paper. Brush the top with egg wash using a gentle dabbing motion [6]. Sprinkle the piped choux with sesame seeds [7].

8. Bake at 191°C/375°F for about 12 minutes until the choux are puffed up. Reduce the temperature to 177°C/350°F and bake for another 10 minutes until the choux are golden brown. Turn off the oven and leave the choux in the oven undisturbed for another 8 minutes. Remove the baked choux from the oven and let cool completely [8].

Soy and Ginger Mousse:

Combine all ingredients for the soy and ginger mousse in a measuring cup and mix well [9]. Pour the mixture through a small fine mesh strainer into the siphon whip bottle [10]. Screw on the top [11] and chill the mixture in the refrigerator for at least an hour before using.

Seared Ahi Tuna:

1. Cut the tuna into large rectangle pieces [12]. In a small bowl, combine soy sauce, fresh ginger, honey, wasabi paste, sesame oil, and orange zest. Mix well [13].

2. Place the tuna pieces in a plastic bag or large container. Coat the tuna with the marinating mixture [14, 15]. Allow the tuna to marinate for about 2 hours in the refrigerator.

3. Remove the tuna from the refrigerator about 30 minutes before cooking. Remove the tuna from the marinating mixture and pat dry with paper towels. Coat the tuna with sesame seeds on all sides and set aside [16].

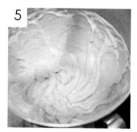

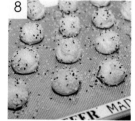

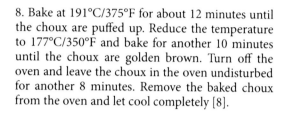

4. Meanwhile, heat the oil in a large stainless steel sauté pan over medium-high heat. When the oil reaches about 200°C/392°F [17], carefully place the tuna in the pan. Quickly sear the tuna on all sides [18].

Assembly and Decoration:

1. Insert the N_2O charger into the siphon whip [19]. Shake the bottle vigorously. Attach the large whip injector to the siphon whip [20]. Inject the sesame choux with the soy and ginger mousse [21, 22].

2. Cut the seared tuna into small cubes. Attach the tuna pieces and soy-ginger-filled choux to bamboo skewers [23] and serve.

LIST OF RESOURCES

I think the best method for locating hard-to-find ingredients and baking tools is to conduct an internet search. For your reference, I have included a list of the stores where I shopped for the ingredients and tools used in this book.

For Pastry Equipment and Tools:

Amazon.com (www.amazon.com)
Chef Rubber (www.chefrubber.com)
JB Prince (www.jbprince.com)
Kerekes (www.bakedeco.com)
King Arthur Flour (www.kingarthurflour.com)
Pastry Chef Central (www.pastrychef.com)
Sur la Table (www.surlatable.com)
Williams-Sonoma (www.williams-sonoma.com)

For Pastry Ingredients:

Adagio Teas (www.adagio.com): loose tea leaves
Amazon.com (www.amazon.com): general pastry ingredients
American Almond Products Company (www.americanalmond.com): wholes nuts and nut flours
Arizona Vanilla Company (www.arizonavanilla.com): vanilla beans
Chef Rubber (www.chefrubber.com): general pastry ingredients, powdered food coloring
The Chefs' Warehouse (www.chefswarehouse.com): general pastry ingredients
Honeyville Food Products (www.honeyvillegrain.com): almond flours, dried egg whites
King Arthur Flour (www.kingarthurflour.com): general pastry ingredients
L'Epicerie (www.lepicerie.com): fruit purees
Marky's (www.markys.com): fruit purees
Pastry Chef Central (www.pastrychef.com): general pastry ingredients
Teavana (www.teavana.com): loose tea leaves
World Wide Chocolate (www.worldwidechocolate.com): chocolates

ALSO AVAILABLE

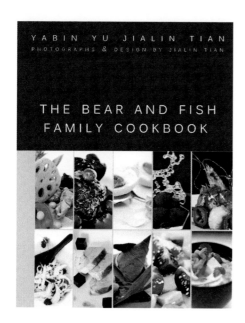

CPSIA information can be obtained
at www.ICGtesting.com
Printed in the USA
BVXC01n1534051214
378072BV00005B/16